DO INFECTIOUS DISEASES POSE A SERIOUS THREAT?

Other books in the At Issue series:

DO INFECTIOUS DISEASES POSE A SERIOUS THREAT?

Viqi Wagner, *Book Editor*

Bruce Glassman, *Vice President*
Bonnie Szumski, *Publisher*
Helen Cothran, *Managing Editor*

GREENHAVEN PRESS
An imprint of Thomson Gale, a part of The Thomson Corporation

Detroit • New York • San Francisco • San Diego • New Haven, Conn.
Waterville, Maine • London • Munich

LIBRARY OF CONGRESS CATALOGING-IN-PUBLICATION DATA

Do infectious diseases pose a serious threat? / Viqi Wagner, book editor.
    p. cm. — (At issue)
  Includes bibliographical references and index.
  ISBN 0-7377-2330-0 (lib. : alk. paper) — ISBN 0-7377-2331-9 (pbk. : alk. paper)
    1. Communicable diseases—Popular works. 2. Public health—Popular works.
3. Emerging infectious diseases—Popular works. 4. Epidemiology—Popular
works. I. Wagner, Viqi, 1953– . II. At issue (San Diego, Calif.)
  RA643.D595 2005
  614.4—dc22   2004040582

#54081568

Contents

Introduction

Microbes have existed for hundreds of millions of years, occupying every conceivable ecological niche on Earth. The vast majority are essential to animal and plant life. However, a minority of microbes, defined as pathogenic, cause acute infectious disease or trigger chronic disease in humans. Historically, the consequences have been devastating—medieval plague epidemics killed one-third of the population of Europe, and at the start of the twentieth century tuberculosis, diarrheal diseases, and pneumonia caused 30 percent of all deaths in the United States.

Twentieth-century technological, medical, and public health advances, hailed as "magic bullets," seemed to promise an end to this threat to human health. Improvements in urban sanitation, cleaner water supplies, and especially the introduction of antibiotics and vaccines led to predictions that the scourge of infectious disease was at an end. Indeed, the World Health Organization declared the eradication of smallpox in 1980. In the United States annual deaths from infectious disease had dropped from 797 to 36 per 100,000 persons and the average life expectancy had increased from 47 in 1900 to 76 in 1980.

A 2003 report by the Institute of Medicine of the National Academy of Sciences outlines policy changes in the United States stemming from such exhilarating success:

> As a result of this apparent reprieve from infectious diseases, the United States government moved research funding away from infectious disease toward the "new dimensions" of public health—noncommunicable diseases such as heart disease and lung cancer. The government closed "virtually every tropical and infectious disease outpost run by the U.S. military and Public Health Service." . . . Infectious disease surveillance and control activities were deemphasized. Research, development, and production of new antibiotics and vaccines declined. The potentially devastating impact of infectious diseases was either relegated to the memory of previous generations or left to the imagination of science-fiction enthusiasts. Americans could all look forward to long, healthy lives, free from infectious disease . . . or could they?

Unfortunately, they could not. Since 1980, optimistic scenarios have been replaced by grim statistics, particularly in developing countries. The World Health Organization reports that today infectious disease is responsible for half of all deaths in developing countries, and is the leading cause of death in children and young adults. Worldwide, 90 percent of infectious disease deaths are due to respiratory infections, AIDS, diarrheal diseases, tuberculosis, malaria, and measles. Moreover, more than thirty previously unknown or reemerging infectious diseases have been identi-

7

fied since 1970. Public health agencies and medical researchers are raising alarms about the worsening threat of infectious diseases and the inadequacy of resources to combat the threat.

According to medical researchers and epidemiologists, a number of factors make the present-day control and treatment of infectious diseases extremely difficult. Many of these factors played a role in the 2003 outbreak of severe acute respiratory syndrome, or SARS, the first severe, easily transmissible new infectious disease of the twenty-first century and a good example of the challenges posed by infectious disease in the modern world.

First, human encroachment into undeveloped regions, for living space and for natural resources, exposes people to previously unidentified microbes against which they have no immunity. In particular, animal-to-human transmission of microbes that are not harmful to their animal hosts but may be lethal to humans has been cited as a major source of emerging diseases. Researchers believe SARS originated in remote areas of China's Guangdong province, where exotic-animal dealers capture civet cats for Chinese urban markets. A strain of the SARS virus has been identified in civet cats, and species jumping is suspected.

The spread of infectious disease originating in animal species depends not only on how easily animals transmit the microbe to humans but also on how easily one infected human can transmit the microbe to another human. That likelihood has increased exponentially because of modern patterns of rapid transportation and increasing population density. Agricultural goods and people now cross the globe in a matter of hours, and international travel has become more affordable than ever before. Thus in a mobile, interconnected world, pathogens can be spread quickly, especially if there is a long incubation period before symptoms appear. In the spring of 2003 the average incubation period for the SARS virus was only two to seven days, and yet failure to identify and quarantine infected individuals has been blamed for the spread of the disease from China to Vietnam to Singapore to Canada, and ultimately to six continents, in a matter of three months. SARS spread most rapidly in big cities; logically, the risk of infection is higher wherever a single infected person may come in contact with hundreds of other people every day.

In the case of emerging diseases, rapid transmission hampers the medical response simply because it is time-consuming, costly, and difficult to diagnose an unknown pathogen and begin effective treatment, if indeed effective treatment exists. The diagnosis of SARS was a success story. The first clinical cases of SARS appeared in China in November 2002, but SARS did not attract international attention until its severity and transmissibility were recognized in March 2003. Confirmed diagnosis of the coronavirus that causes SARS came in mid-April, along with news that effective antibiotics existed to combat the disease. Diagnosis was not simple, however; the early symptoms of SARS mimic harmless flulike symptoms for which most people are not likely to seek medical attention, raising fears that very dangerous diseases such as SARS may go unnoticed until it is too late to control their spread.

The existence of effective drugs to treat SARS was atypical. Researchers point to a dwindling number of effective drug treatments and a lack of preventive vaccines as a major factor in the growing threat of infectious diseases. There are no vaccines for the host of emerging diseases identified since 1980, including AIDS, tuberculosis, and malaria, pandemics that together account for 500 million illnesses a year and at least 6 million deaths. Moreover, recent awareness of biological agents as possible weapons of terrorism has focused attention on public vulnerability to smallpox. The last smallpox vaccination program in the United States, for example, ended in 1972; immunity to the disease wears off approximately ten years after vaccination, and since the September 11, 2001, terrorist attacks the U.S. government has scrambled to make enough smallpox vaccine to reimmunize the general public in case of a biological attack.

The biggest treatment-related problem concerns growing microbial resistance to existing antibiotics. Through natural mutation and overuse of antibiotics, which encourages the growth of resistant strains of pathogens, many microbes once destroyed by a wide range of drugs are now resistant to all known antibiotics. According to a 1997 Institute of Medicine study, in the United States up to 35 percent of *Streptococcus pneumonia* infections are resistant to penicillin, 32 percent of *Staphylococcus aureus* infections do not respond to the once-powerful antibiotic methicillin, and 13 percent of tuberculosis infections are resistant to all drug therapies.

Critics charge that the world's public health infrastructures, under scrutiny as epidemics rage, are too weak to respond effectively to infectious disease outbreaks. Electronic reporting systems and databases have been instrumental in tracking the spread of disease, but containing and controlling disease is much more challenging to underfunded, underequipped public health agencies, especially where political instability or censorship restricts the timely spread of information.

In 2003, for example, Chinese public health officials at first failed to release news of SARS to the Chinese public, failed to accurately report cases of SARS to international health agencies, and failed to take steps to protect health-care workers in time to prevent additional infections. In turn, immigration controls failed to identify those who had contact with sick people in time to prevent them from exposing others across international borders. In affected countries, sketchy news of a new, deadly epidemic fueled signs of public hysteria—thousands, for example, began wearing face masks—and media exaggeration.

Eventually, with quarantine measures and prompt treatment, the SARS epidemic subsided in the summer of 2003. Public health agencies taking stock of their ability to respond to infectious diseases also tried to prepare for future SARS outbreaks, which some researchers suggest are likely to occur seasonally, like influenza. Generally that assessment has been followed by requests for increased government funding to buy drugs, increases in staff, strengthened laboratory and epidemiological capacities, and public-information campaigns.

Where the next major outbreaks will occur, how to apply resources most effectively to treat current epidemics, and how to reduce the threat of infectious disease are subjects of intense debate. The articles in *At Issue: Do Infectious Diseases Pose a Serious Threat?* examine the scope of the problem. Meanwhile, China reported in January 2004 the first three cases of a new outbreak of SARS.

1

The Global Threat of Infectious Diseases: An Overview

National Intelligence Council

The National Intelligence Council (NIC) is an advisory group within the U.S. Department of State. In addition to producing classified analyses of current foreign policy issues for internal government use, the NIC also researches broad global trends in science, technology, and the environment and publishes its findings in unclassified National Intelligence Estimates.

Infectious diseases pose a major danger to human health, accounting for one-fourth to one-third of worldwide deaths annually. Most of the deadliest of known infectious diseases are either spreading or becoming drug resistant, and dozens of previously unknown diseases have emerged since the 1970s. Particularly in developing countries, where health care and government funding are limited and where malnutrition and poor water quality are rampant, infectious diseases have an enormously disruptive social, economic, and political impact. Antibiotic resistance; lack of replacement drugs; the continued spread of HIV, TB, and malaria; and persistent poverty in the developing world will intensify the crisis in the years ahead. Between 2010 and 2020, however, experts guardedly predict that medical advances, socioeconomic development, and improved disease surveillance and control are likely to reduce the threat.

Broad advances in controlling or eradicating a growing number of infectious diseases—such as tuberculosis (TB), malaria, and smallpox—in the decades after the Second World War—fueled hopes that the global infectious disease threat would be increasingly manageable. Optimism regarding the battle against infectious diseases peaked in 1978 when the United Nations (UN) member states signed the "Health for All 2000" accord, which predicted that even the poorest nations would undergo a

National Intelligence Council, "The Global Infectious Disease Threat and Its Implication for the United States," U.S. Department of State, *NIE 99-17D*, January 2000.

health transition before the millennium, whereby infectious diseases no longer would pose a major danger to human health. As recently as 1996, a World Bank/World Health Organization (WHO)–sponsored study by Christopher J.L. Murray and Alan D. Lopez projected a dramatic reduction in the infectious disease threat. This optimism, however, led to complacency and overlooked the role of such factors as expanded trade and travel and growing microbial resistance to existing antibiotics in the spread of infectious diseases. Today:

- Infectious diseases remain a leading cause of death. Of the estimated 54 million deaths worldwide in 1998, about one-fourth to one-third were due to infectious diseases, most of them in developing countries and among children globally. . . .
- Although there has been continuing progress in controlling some vaccine-preventable childhood diseases such as polio, neonatal tetanus, and measles, a White House–appointed interagency working group identified at least 29 previously unknown diseases that have appeared globally since 1973, many of them incurable, including HIV/AIDS, Ebola hemorrhagic fever, and hepatitis C. [In 1999] Nipah encephalitis was identified in Malaysia. Twenty well-known diseases such as malaria, TB, cholera, and dengue have rebounded after a period of decline or spread to new regions, often in deadlier forms.
- These trends are reflected in the United States as well, where annual infectious disease deaths have nearly doubled to some 170,000 since 1980 after reaching historic lows that year, while new and existing pathogens, such as HIV and West Nile virus, respectively, continue to enter US borders.

The deadly seven

The seven infectious diseases that caused the highest number of deaths in 1998, according to WHO and [the Defense Intelligence Agency's] Armed Forces Medical Intelligence Center (AFMIC), will remain threats well into the [twenty-first] century. HIV/AIDS, TB, malaria, and hepatitis B and C are either spreading or becoming more drug-resistant, while lower respiratory infections, diarrheal diseases, and measles, appear to have at least temporarily peaked.

At least 29 previously unknown diseases . . . have appeared globally since 1973, many of them incurable.

Following its identification in 1983, the spread of HIV intensified quickly. Despite progress in some regions, HIV/AIDS shows no signs of abating globally. Approximately 2.3 million people died from AIDS worldwide in 1998, up dramatically from 0.7 million in 1993, and there were 5.8 million new infections. According to WHO, some 33.4 million people were living with HIV by 1998, up from 10 million in 1990, and the number could approach 40 million by the end of 2000. Although infection and death rates have slowed considerably in developed countries owing to the growing use of preventive measures and costly new multidrug treatment therapies, the pandemic continues to spread in much of the developing world, where 95 percent of global infections and deaths have occurred. Sub-Saharan Africa currently has the biggest regional burden, but the disease is spreading quickly in India, Russia, China, and much of the rest of Asia. HIV/AIDS probably will cause more deaths than any other single infectious disease worldwide by 2020 and may account for up to one-half or more of infectious disease deaths in the developing world alone.

Twenty well-known diseases such as malaria, TB, cholera, and dengue have rebounded after a period of decline or spread to new regions, often in deadlier forms.

WHO declared TB a global emergency in 1993 and the threat continues to grow, especially from multidrug resistant TB. The disease is especially prevalent in Russia, India, Southeast Asia, Sub-Saharan Africa, and parts of Latin America. More than 1.5 million people died of TB in 1998, excluding those infected with HIV/AIDS, and there were up to 7.4 million new cases. Although the vast majority of TB infections and deaths occur in developing regions, the disease also is encroaching into developed regions due to increased immigration and travel and less emphasis on prevention. Drug resistance is a growing problem; . . . WHO has reported that up to 50 percent of people with multidrug resistant TB may die of their infection despite treatment, which can be 10 to 50 times more expensive than that used for drug-sensitive TB. HIV/AIDS also has contributed to the resurgence of TB. One-quarter of the increase in TB incidence involves co-infection with HIV. TB probably will rank second only to HIV/AIDS as a cause of infectious disease deaths by 2020.

Malaria, a mainly tropical disease that seemed to be coming under control in the 1960s and 1970s, is making a deadly comeback—especially in Sub-Saharan Africa where infection rates increased by 40 percent from 1970 to 1997. Drug resistance, historically a problem only with the most severe form of the disease, is now increasingly reported in the milder variety, while the prospects for an effective vaccine are poor. In 1998, an estimated 300 million people were infected with malaria, and more than 1.1 million died from the disease that year. Most of the deaths occurred in Sub-Saharan Africa. According to the U.S. Agency for International Development (USAID), Sub-Saharan Africa alone is likely to experience a 7- to 20-percent annual increase in malaria-related deaths and severe illnesses over the next several years.

Hepatitis B, which caused at least 0.6 million deaths in 1997, is highly endemic in the developing world, and some 350 million people worldwide are chronic carriers. The less prevalent but far more lethal hepatitis C identified in 1989 has grown dramatically and is a significant contributor to cirrhosis and liver cancer. WHO estimated that 3 percent of the global population was infected with the hepatitis C virus by 1997, which means that more than 170 million people were at risk of developing the diseases associated with this virus. Various studies project that up to 25 percent of people with chronic hepatitis B and C will die of cirrhosis of the liver and liver cancer over the next 20 to 30 years.

Lower respiratory infections, especially influenza and pneumonia, killed 3.5 million people in 1998, most of them children in developing countries, down from 4.1 million in 1993. Owing to immunosuppression from malnutrition and growing microbial resistance to commonly used drugs such as penicillin, these children are especially vulnerable to such diseases and will continue to experience high death rates.

Diarrheal diseases—mainly spread by contaminated water or food—accounted for 2.2 million deaths in 1998, as compared to 3 million in 1993, of which about 60 percent occurred among children under five years of age in developing countries. The most common cause of death related to diarrheal diseases is infection with *Escherichia coli*. Other diarrheal diseases include cholera, dysentery, and rotaviral diarrhea, prevalent throughout the developing world and, more recently, in many former communist states. Such waterborne and foodborne diseases will remain highly prevalent in these regions in the absence of improvements in water quality and sanitation.

HIV/AIDS probably will cause more deaths than any other single infectious disease worldwide by 2020.

Despite substantial progress against measles in recent years, the disease still infects some 42 million children annually and killed about 0.9 million in 1998, down from 1.2 million in 1993. It is a leading cause of death among refugees and internally displaced persons during complex humanitarian emergencies. Measles will continue to pose a major threat in developing countries, particularly Sub-Saharan Africa, until the still relatively low vaccination rates are substantially increased. It also will continue to cause periodic epidemics in areas such as South America with higher, but still inadequate, vaccination rates. . . .

Regional trends

The overall level of global health care capacity has improved substantially in recent decades, but in most poorer countries the availability of various types of health care—ranging from basic pharmaceuticals and postnatal care to costly multidrug therapies—remains very limited. Almost all research and development funds allocated by developed country governments and pharmaceutical companies, moreover, are focused on advancing therapies and drugs relevant to developed country maladies, and those that are relevant to developing country needs usually are beyond their financial reach. This is generating a growing controversy between rich and poorer nations over such issues as intellectual property rights, as some developing countries seek to meet their pharmaceutical needs with locally produced generic products. Malnutrition, poor sanitation, and poor water quality in developing countries also will continue to add to the disease burden that is overwhelming health care infrastructures in many countries. So too, will political instability and conflict and the reluctance of many governments to confront issues such as the spread of HIV/AIDS. . . .

Sub-Saharan Africa will remain the region most affected by the global infectious disease phenomenon—accounting for nearly half of infectious disease-caused deaths worldwide. Deaths from HIV/AIDS, malaria, cholera, and several lesser known diseases exceed those in all other regions. Sixty-five percent of all deaths in Sub-Saharan Africa are caused by infectious diseases. Rudimentary health care delivery and response systems, the unavailability or misuse of drugs, the lack of funds, and the multiplicity of conflicts are exacerbating the crisis. . . . Investment in health care in the region is minimal, less than 40 percent of the people in countries such as Nigeria and the Democratic Republic of the Congo (DROC) have access to basic medical care, and even in relatively well off South Africa, only 50 to 70 percent have such access, with black populations at the low end of the spectrum.

Four-fifths of all HIV-related deaths and 70 percent of new infections worldwide in 1998 occurred in the region, totaling 1.8–2 million and 4 million, respectively. Although only a tenth of the world's population lives in the region, 11.5 million of 13.9 million cumulative AIDS deaths have occurred there. Eastern and southern African countries, including South Africa, are the worst affected, with 10 to 26 percent of adults infected with the disease. Sub-Saharan Africa has high TB prevalence, as well as the highest HIV/TB co-infection rate, with TB deaths totaling 0.55 million in 1998. The hardest hit countries are in equatorial and especially southern Africa. South Africa, in particular, is facing the biggest increase in the region.

Sub-Saharan Africa accounts for an estimated 90 percent of the global malaria burden. Ten percent of the regional disease burden is attributed to malaria, with roughly 1 million deaths in 1998. Cholera, dysentery, and other diarrheal diseases also are major killers in the region, particularly among children, refugees, and internally displaced populations. Forty percent of all childhood deaths from diarrheal diseases occur in Sub-Saharan Africa. The region also has a high rate of hepatitis B and C infections and is the only region with a perennial meningococcal meningitis problem in a "meningitis belt" stretching from west to east. Sub-Saharan Africa also suffers from yellow fever, while trypanasomiasis or "sleeping sickness" is making a comeback in the DROC and Sudan, and the Marburg virus also appeared in DROC for the first time in 1998. Ebola hemorrhagic fever strikes sporadically in countries such as the DROC, Gabon, Cote d'Ivoire, and Sudan.

Asia and the Pacific

Although the more developed countries of Asia and the Pacific, such as Japan, South Korea, Australia, and New Zealand, have strong records in combating infectious diseases, infectious disease prevalence in South and Southeast Asia is almost as high as in Sub-Saharan Africa. The health care delivery system of the Asia and Pacific region—the majority of which is privately financed—is particularly vulnerable to economic downturns even though this is offset to some degree by much of the region's reliance on traditional medicine from local practitioners. According to the AFMIC typology, 90 to 100 percent of the populations in the most developed countries, such as Japan and Australia, have access to high-quality health care. Forty to 50 percent have such access among the large populations of China and South Asia, while southeast Asian health care is more varied, with less than 40 percent enjoying such access in Burma and Cambodia, and 50 to 70 percent in Thailand, Malaysia, and the Philippines. In South and Southeast Asia, reemergent diseases such as TB, malaria, cholera, and dengue fever are rampant, while HIV/AIDS, after a late start, is growing faster than in any other region. . . .

Latin America and Europe

Latin American countries are making considerable progress in infectious disease control, including the eradication of polio and major reductions in the incidence and death rates of measles, neonatal tetanus, some diarrheal diseases, and acute respiratory infections. Nonetheless, infectious diseases are still a major cause of illness and death in the region, and the risk of new and reemerging diseases remains substantial. Widening income disparities, periodic economic shocks, and rampant urbanization have disrupted disease control efforts and contributed to widespread reemergence of cholera, malaria, TB, and dengue, especially in the poorer Central American and Caribbean countries and in the Amazon basin of South America. . . . Latin America's health care capacity is substantially more advanced than that of Sub-Saharan Africa and somewhat better than mainland Asia's, with 70 to 90 percent of populations having access to basic health care in Chile, Costa Rica, and Cuba on the upper end of the scale. Less than 50 percent have such access in Haiti, most of Central America, and the Amazon basin countries, including the rural populations in Brazil. . . .

Sub-Saharan Africa will remain the region most affected by the global infectious disease phenomenon—accounting for nearly half of infectious disease-related deaths worldwide.

The sharp decline in health care infrastructure in Russia and elsewhere in the former Soviet Union (FSU) and, to a lesser extent, in Eastern Europe—owing to economic difficulties—are causing a dramatic rise in infectious disease incidence. Death rates attributed to infectious diseases in the FSU increased 50 percent from 1990 to 1996, with TB accounting for a substantial number of such deaths. . . . Access to health care ranges from 50 to 70 percent in most European FSU states, including Russia and Ukraine, and from 40 to 50 percent in FSU states located in Central Asia. This is generally supported by WHO estimates indicating that only 50 to 80 percent of FSU citizens had regular access to essential drugs in 1997, as compared to more than 95 percent a decade earlier as health care budgets and government-provided health services were slashed. Access to health care is generally better in Eastern Europe, particularly in more developed states such as Poland, the Czech Republic, and Hungary, where it ranges from 70 to 90 percent, while only 50 to 70 percent have access in countries such as Bulgaria and Romania. More than 95 percent of the population throughout the East European region had such access in 1987, according to WHO.

Crowded living conditions are among the causes fueling a TB epidemic in the FSU, especially among prison populations—while surging intravenous drug use and rampant prostitution are substantially responsible for a marked increase in HIV/AIDS incidence. There were 111,000 new TB infections in Russia alone in 1996, a growing number of them multidrug resistant, and nearly 25,000 deaths due to TB—numbers that could increase significantly following periodic releases of prisoners to relieve overcrowding. . . .

[Western Europe's] highly developed health care infrastructure and delivery system tend to limit the incidence and especially the death rates of most infectious diseases, though not the economic costs.

Western Europe faces threats from a number of emerging and reemerging infectious diseases such as HIV/AIDS, TB, and hepatitis B and C, as well as several zoonotic [passed from animal to human] diseases. Its status as a hub of international travel, commerce, and immigration, moreover, dramatically increases the risks of importing new diseases from other regions. Tens of millions of West Europeans travel to developing countries annually, increasing the prospects for the importation of dangerous diseases, as demonstrated by the importation of typhoid in 1999. Some 88 percent of regional population growth in the first half of the decade was due to immigration; legal immigrants now comprise about 6 percent of the population, and illegal newcomers number an estimated 6 million. Nonetheless, the region's highly developed health care infrastructure and delivery system tend to limit the incidence and especially the death rates of most infectious diseases, though not the economic costs. Access to high-quality care is available throughout most of the region, although governments are beginning to limit some heretofore generous health benefits, and a growing antivaccination movement in parts of Western Europe, such as Germany, is causing a rise in measles and other vaccine-preventable diseases. . . . The region as a whole is ranked in the highest category, along with North America.

After increasing sharply for most of the 1980s and 1990s, HIV infections, and particularly HIV/AIDS deaths, have slowed considerably owing to behavioral changes among high-risk populations and the availability and funding for multidrug treatment. Some 0.5 million people were living with HIV/AIDS in 1998, down slightly from 510,000 the preceding year, and there were 30,000 new cases and 12,000 deaths, with prevalence somewhat higher in much of southern Europe than in the north. TB, especially its multidrug resistant strains, is on the upswing, as is co-infection with HIV, particularly in the larger countries, with some 50,000 TB cases reported in 1996. Hepatitis C prevalence is growing, especially in southern Europe. Western Europe also continues to suffer from several zoonotic diseases, among which is the deadly new variant Creutzfeldt-Jakob disease (nvCJD), linked to the bovine spongiform encephalopathy or "mad cow disease" outbreak in the United Kingdom in 1995 that has since ebbed following implementation of strict control measures. Other recent disease concerns include meningococcal meningitis outbreaks in the Benelux countries and leishmaniasis-HIV co-infection, especially in southern Europe. . . .

The outlook for infectious diseases until 2020

The impact of infectious diseases [from 2000 to 2020] will be heavily influenced by three sets of variables. The first is the relationship between increasing microbial resistance and scientific efforts to develop new antibiotics and vaccines. The second is the trajectory of developing and transitional economies, especially concerning the basic quality of life of the poorest groups in these countries. The third is the degree of success of global and national efforts to create effective systems of surveillance and response. The interplay of these drivers will determine the overall outlook.

On the positive side, reduced fertility and the aging of the population, continued economic development, and improved health care capacity in many countries, especially the more developed, will increase the progress toward a health transition by 2020 whereby the impact of infectious diseases ebbs, as compared to noninfectious diseases. On the negative side, continued rapid population growth, urbanization, and persistent poverty in much of the developing world, and the paradox in which some aspects of socioeconomic development—such as increased trade and travel—actually foster the spread of infectious diseases, could slow or derail that transition. So, too, will growing microbial resistance among resurgent diseases, such as malaria and TB, and the proliferation or intensification of new ones, such as HIV/AIDS. . . .

> *The impact of infectious diseases [from 2000 to 2020] will be heavily influenced by . . . the relationship between . . . microbial resistance and scientific efforts to develop new antibiotics and vaccines.*

According to [the most likely] scenario, continued deterioration [from 2000 to 2010]—led by hard core killers such as HIV/AIDS, TB, and malaria—is followed by limited improvement [from 2010 to 2020] owing primarily to gains against childhood and vaccine-preventable diseases such as diarrheal diseases, neonatal tetanus, and measles. The scale and scope of the overall infectious disease threat diminishes, but the remaining threat consists of especially deadly or incurable diseases such as HIV/AIDS, TB, hepatitis C and possibly, heretofore, unknown diseases, with HIV/AIDS and TB likely comprising the overwhelming majority of infectious disease deaths in developing countries alone by 2020. . . .

We are likely to witness neither steady progress against the infectious disease threat nor its unabated intensification. Instead, progress is likely to be slow and uneven, with advances, such as the recent development of a new type of antibiotic drug against certain hospital-acquired infections, frequently offset by renewed setbacks, such as new signs of growing microbial resistance among available HIV/AIDS drugs and withdrawal of a promising new vaccine against rotavirus because of adverse side effects. On balance, negative drivers, such as microbial resistance, are likely to prevail [until 2010], but given time, positive ones, such as gradual socioeconomic development and improved health care capacity, will likely come to the fore [between 2010 and 2020.] . . .

Persistent poverty in much of the developing world, growing microbial resistance and a dearth of new replacement drugs, inadequate disease surveillance and control capacity, and the high prevalence and continued spread of major killers such as HIV/AIDS, TB, and malaria are likely to remain ascendant and worsen the overall problem during the first half of our time frame. Sub-Saharan Africa, India, and Southeast Asia will remain the hardest hit by these diseases. The European FSU states and China are likely to experience a surge in HIV/AIDS and related diseases such as TB. The developed countries will be threatened principally by the real possibility of a resurgence of the HIV/AIDS threat owing to growing microbial resistance to the current spectrum of multidrug therapies and to a wide array of other drugs used to combat infectious diseases.

> *We are likely to witness neither steady progress against the infectious disease threat nor its unabated intensification.*

Aging populations, global socioeconomic development, improved health care capacity, and medical advances are likely to come to the fore during the second half of our time frame in all but the least developed countries, and even the least developed will experience a measure of improvement.

Aging populations and expected continued declines in fertility throughout Asia, Latin America, the former FSU states, and Sub-Saharan Africa will sharply reduce the size of age cohorts that are particularly susceptible to infectious diseases owing to environmental or behavioral factors.

Socioeconomic development, however fitful, and resulting improvements in water quality, sanitation, nutrition, and education in most developing countries will enable the most susceptible population cohorts to better withstand infectious diseases both physically and behaviorally.

The worsening infectious disease threat we posit for the first decade of our time frame is likely to further energize the international community and most countries to devote more attention and resources to improved infectious disease surveillance, response, and control capacity. The WHO's new campaign against malaria, recent developed country consideration of tying debt forgiveness for the poorest countries in part to their undertaking stronger commitments to combat disease, self-initiated efforts by Sub-Saharan African governments to confront HIV/AIDS, and greater pharmaceutical industry willingness to provide more drugs to poor countries at affordable prices are likely to be harbingers of more such efforts as the infectious disease threat becomes more acute.

The likely eventual approval of new drugs and vaccines—now in the developmental stage—for major killers such as dengue, diarrheal diseases, and possibly even malaria will further ease the infectious disease burden and help counter the microbial resistance phenomenon.

The persistent infectious disease burden is likely to aggravate and . . . may even provoke social fragmentation, economic decay, and political polarization in the hardest hit countries.

Together, these developments are likely to set the stage for at least a limited improvement in infectious disease control, particularly against childhood and vaccine-preventable diseases, such as respiratory infections, diarrheal diseases, neonatal tetanus, and measles in most developing and former communist countries. Given time—and barring the appearance of a deadly and highly infectious new disease, a catastrophic expansion of the HIV/AIDS pandemic, or the release of a highly contagious biological agent capable of rapid and widescale secondary spread—such medical advances, behavioral changes, and improving national and international surveillance and response capacities will eventually produce substantial gains against the overall infectious disease threat. In the event that HIV/AIDS takes a catastrophic turn for the worse in both developed and developing countries, . . . all bets are off.

Economic, social, and political impacts

The persistent infectious disease burden is likely to aggravate and, in extreme cases, may even provoke social fragmentation, economic decay, and political polarization in the hardest hit countries in the developing and former communist worlds in particular. . . . This, in turn, will hamper progress against infectious diseases. Even under the most likely scenario, . . . new and reemergent infectious diseases are likely to have a disruptive impact on global economic, social, and political dynamics.

The macroeconomic costs of the infectious disease burden are increasingly significant for the most seriously affected countries despite the partially offsetting impact of declines in population growth, and they will take an even greater toll on productivity, profitability, and foreign investment in the future. A senior World Bank official considers AIDS to be the single biggest threat to economic development in Sub-Saharan Africa. A growing number of studies suggest that AIDS and malaria alone will reduce GDP [gross domestic production] in several Sub-Saharan African countries by 20 percent or more by 2010. . . .

Infectious diseases will continue to cause costly periodic disruptions in trade and commerce in every region of the world.

- *Avian flu in Hong Kong.* The avian influenza outbreak in 1997 cost the former colony hundreds of millions of dollars in lost poultry production, commerce, and tourism, with airport arrivals in November of that year alone down by 22 percent from the preceding year.

- *BSE and nvCJD in Britain.* The outbreak of BSE and new variant Creutzfeldt-Jakob disease in the United Kingdom in 1995 prompted a mass slaughter of cattle, drastically cut beef consumption, and led to the imposition of a three-year EU embargo against British beef. The losses to the British economy were estimated by the WHO at $5.75 billion, including $2 billion in lost beef exports.
- *Cyclospora in Guatemalan raspberries.* The outbreak of cyclospora-related illness in the United States and Canada associated with raspberries from Guatemala led to curbs in imports that cost Guatemala several million dollars in lost revenue.
- *Cholera in Peru.* The outbreak of cholera in 1991 cost the Peruvian fishing industry an estimated $775 million in lost tourism and trade because of a temporary ban on seafood exports.
- *Foot and mouth disease in Taiwan.* In 1997 an outbreak of foot and mouth disease (FMD) devastated Taiwan's pork industry—one of the largest in the world—shutting down exports for a full year.
- *Nipah in Malaysia.* In 1999, the Nipah virus caused the shutdown of over half of the country's pig farms and an embargo against pork exports.
- *Plague in India.* The plague outbreak in Surat, India, in 1994 and ensuing panic sparked a sudden exodus of 0.5 million people from the region and led to abrupt shutdowns of entire industries, including aviation, and tourism, as several countries froze trade, banned travel from India, and sent some Indian migrants home. The WHO estimated the outbreak cost India some $2 billion.

Fiscal impact

Infectious diseases will increase pressure on national health bills that already consume some 7 to 14 percent of GDP in developed countries, up to 5 percent in the better off developing countries, but currently less than 2 percent in least developed states.

By 2000, the cumulative direct and indirect costs of AIDS alone are likely to have topped $500 billion, according to estimates by the Global AIDS Policy Coalition at Harvard University. In Latin America, the Pan-American Health Organization in 1994 estimated it would take a decade and $200 billion to bring the cholera pandemic in the region under control through a massive water cleanup effort, or nearly 80 percent of total developing country health spending for that year. The direct costs of fighting malaria in Sub-Saharan Africa increased from $800 million in 1989 to $2.2 billion in 1997, largely owing to the far higher cost of treating the growing number of drug-resistant cases, and the trend toward higher costs is likely to continue.

AIDS, along with TB and malaria—particularly the drug-resistant varieties—makes large budgetary claims on national health systems resources. Policy choices will continue to be required along at least three dimensions: spending for health versus spending for other objectives; spending more on prevention in order to spend less on treatment; and treating burgeoning AIDS-infected populations versus treating other illnesses. . . .

Disruptive social impact

At least some of the hardest-hit countries, initially in Sub-Saharan Africa and later in other regions, will face a demographic catastrophe as HIV/AIDS and associated diseases reduce human life expectancy dramatically and kill up to a quarter of their populations. . . . This will further impoverish the poor and often the middle class and produce a huge and impoverished orphan cohort unable to cope and vulnerable to exploitation and radicalization.

Until the early 1990s, economic development and improved health care had raised the life expectancy in developing countries to 64 years, with prospects that it would go higher still. The growing number of deaths from new and reemergent diseases such as AIDS, however, will slow or reverse this trend toward longer life spans in heavily affected countries by as much as 30 years or more by 2010, according to the US Census Bureau. For example, life expectancy will be reduced by 30 years in Botswana and Zimbabwe, by 20 years in Nigeria and South Africa, by 13 years in Honduras, by eight years in Brazil, by four years in Haiti, and by three years in Thailand.

The degradation of nuclear and extended families across all classes will produce severe social and economic dislocations with political consequences, as well. Nearly 35 million children in 27 countries will have lost one or both parents to AIDS by 2000; by 2010, this number will increase to 41.6 million. Nineteen of the hardest hit countries are in Sub-Saharan Africa, where HIV/AIDS has been prevalent across all social sectors. Children are increasingly acquiring HIV from their mothers during pregnancy or through breast-feeding, ensuring prolongation and intensification of the epidemic and its economic reverberations. With as much as a third of the children under 15 in hardest-hit countries expected to comprise a "lost orphaned generation" by 2010 with little hope of educational or employment opportunities, these countries will be at risk of further economic decay, increased crime, and political instability as such young people become radicalized or are exploited by various political groups for their own ends; the pervasive child soldier phenomenon may be one example. . . .

Threats to the United States

As a major hub of global travel, immigration, and commerce, along with having a large civilian and military presence and wide-ranging interests overseas, the United States will remain at risk from global infectious disease outbreaks, or even a bioterrorist incident using infectious disease microbes. Infectious diseases will continue to kill nearly 170,000 Americans annually and many more in the event of an epidemic of influenza or yet-unknown disease or a steep decline in the effectiveness of available HIV/AIDS drugs. Although several emerging infectious diseases, such as HIV/AIDS, were first identified in the United States, most, including HIV/AIDS, originate outside US borders, with the entry of the West Nile virus in 1999 a case in point.

The US civilian population will remain directly vulnerable to a wide variety of infectious diseases, from resurgent ones such as multidrug resistant TB to deadly newer ones such as HIV/AIDS and hepatitis C. Infectious disease-related deaths in the United States have increased by about 4.8 percent per year since 1980 to 59 deaths per 100,000 people by 1996, or roughly 170,000 deaths annually, as compared to an annual decrease of 2.3 percent in the preceding 15 years and an alltime low of 36 deaths per 100,000 in 1980. The USCD [Centers for Disease Control and Prevention] estimates that the total direct and indirect medical costs from infectious diseases comprise some 15 percent of all US health care expenditures or $120 billion in 1995 dollars.

The biological warfare and terrorism threat to US national security is on the rise.

In the opinion of the U.S. Institute of Medicine, the next major infectious disease threat to the United States may be, like HIV, a previously unrecognized pathogen. Barring that, the most likely known infectious diseases to directly and significantly impact the United States over the next decade will be HIV/AIDS, hepatitis C, and multidrug resistant TB, or a new, more lethal variant of influenza. Foodborne illnesses and hospital-acquired infections also pose a threat:

- *HIV/AIDS* was first identified in the United States in 1983 but originated in Sub-Saharan Africa. In the United States, HIV/AIDS deaths surged from 7,000 in 1985 to 50,000 in 1995 before dropping dramatically to 17,000 in 1997 as a result of behavioral and therapeutic changes among the most at risk populations. The total number of those infected reached 890,000 for all of North America in 1998, including 44,000 new infections, most of them in the United States. Although HIV/AIDS-related death rates have declined sharply, the poor prospects that a vaccine will be available over the next decade or more, along with the likelihood that the virus will develop growing resistance to the protease-inhibitor drugs now in use, portend a continued rise in the infection rate and a renewed rise in the death rate.
- *Hepatitis C.* Some 4 million Americans are chronic carriers of hepatitis C, which was first identified in the United States in 1989. The hepatitis C burden will continue to grow for at least another decade due to the disease's long incubation period, with the number of deaths possibly surpassing HIV/AIDS deaths by 2005 even though the rate of new infections is dropping, owing to improved blood supply testing. About 15 percent of those infected will develop life-threatening cirrhosis of the liver, and many more will experience a more slowly developing chronic liver disease, including cancer. The disease also will remain the leading cause of liver transplantation.
- *Foodborne illnesses.* According to the USCDC, tens of millions of foodborne illness cases, including 9,000 deaths, occur each year in the United States. The threat from foodborne illnesses will persist given changing consumption patterns and further globalization of the food supply.
- The threat from highly virulent, antimicrobial-resistant pathogens such as *Staphylococcus aureus*, *Streptococcus pneumoniae*, and *enterro-*

cocci—which kill some 14,000 hospital patients annually—is likely to grow, particularly if the remaining small arsenal of effective drugs, such as vancomycin, becomes ineffective.

- *TB.* After declining dramatically for several decades, TB in the first half of the 1990s made a comeback in urban areas and in some 13 states with large refugee and immigrant populations, where some 23,000 to 27,000 cases were reported annually, up from a low of 22,000 in 1984. More alarming was the rise of multidrug resistant TB from 10 percent of total cases before 1984 to 52 percent of cases resistant to at least one drug and 32 percent resistant to two or more of the five frontline anti-TB drugs a decade later. Some high-risk populations in prisons and those with HIV/AIDS have experienced death rates from TB as high as 70 to 90 percent. Although a massive and costly intervention by state and local authorities reversed the overall infection rate to 18,000 by 1998, the multidrug resistant TB threat persists, and TB incidence continues to grow among immigrant populations. About 40 percent of all active TB cases in the United States—up from 16 percent in 1982—currently occur among immigrants, particularly illegal ones from countries where TB is highly endemic.

- *Influenza.* Although the deadly 1918 influenza pandemic that caused more than 0.5 million US deaths appears to have started in the United States, almost all others have originated in China and Southeast Asia. Epidemiologists generally agree that the threat of another "killer" influenza pandemic is high and that it is not a question of whether, but when, it will occur. Even in the absence of a widespread "killer" pandemic, influenza has caused 30,000 US deaths annually in recent years—nearly double the annual average in the 1972–84 period, owing in part to the high vulnerability to the disease of the growing cohort of older Americans and HIV-infected persons. Influenza will remain essentially an uncontrolled disease because the viruses are highly efficient in their ability to survive and change into more virulent strains. USCDC researchers predict that, in an influenza epidemic infecting 15 percent of the US population, the mean number of expected deaths would be approximately 97,000 in one year, regardless of immunization status. The number of hospitalizations would total 314,000, and the number of outpatient cases would reach 18 million. If the attack rate were 35 percent, the number of expected deaths would be 227,000 in one year and all other illness rates would be correspondingly higher. . . .

- *Malaria.* Malaria was domestically eliminated in the 1960s but has reemerged over the last two decades due to the increase in immigration and international travel. Currently, some 1,200 cases of malaria are reported to the USCDC annually, with about half occurring among US travelers to highly endemic countries in the tropics and the other half among foreign nationals entering the United States, primarily agricultural workers and illegal migrants. Although malaria outbreaks have been relatively isolated and have been brought under control quickly, the disease has the potential to become reestablished in the United States because of the abundance of mosquito vectors, especially in southern states.

- Fears that *cholera*, has become endemic in Latin America over the past decade, would find its way into the United States have not been realized, but isolated cases have been occurring at a more frequent rate than at any time since 1962 when cholera surveillance commenced. Thus, the disease looms as a potential threat.
- *Dengue.* Dengue, along with the far more serious dengue hemorrhagic fever and dengue shock syndrome, was reintroduced into the United States in the mid-1980s by foreign travelers; the mosquito vector is now widespread throughout the southeast. There were 90 cases in 1998, all of which were acquired overseas.
- *Foreign animal diseases.* In addition to the more obvious human impacts, imported animal diseases present considerable potential risks to the domestic economy, trade, and commerce. Those potentially capable of significantly harming US agriculture include foot and mouth disease (FMD), avian influenza, bovine spongiform encephalopathy, and African swine fever. An outbreak of foot and mouth disease in the US livestock industry could cost as much as $20 billion over 15 years in increased consumer costs, reduced livestock productivity, and restricted trade, according to USDA estimates. Another USDA study revealed that, if African swine fever were to become reestablished in the US swine population, the cost over a 10-year period would be $5.4 billion. . . .

The biological warfare threat

The biological warfare and terrorism threat to US national security is on the rise as rogue states and terrorist groups also exploit the ease of global travel and communication in pursuit of their goals.

The ability of such foreign-based groups and individuals to enter and operate within the United States has already been demonstrated and could recur. The West Nile virus scare, and several earlier instances of suspected bioterrorism, showed, as well, the confusion and fear they can sow regardless of whether or not they are validated.

The threat to US forces and interests overseas also will continue to increase as more nations develop a capability to field at least limited numbers of biological weapons, and nihilistic and religiously motivated groups contemplate opting for them to cause maximum casualties.

2

Modern Trends Greatly Increase the Threat of Infectious Diseases

Jennifer Brower and Peter Chalk

Jennifer Brower is a policy analyst at RAND, a nonprofit think tank assisting corporate and government decision makers, in Arlington, Virginia. She holds a PhD in environmental engineering and microbiology from Harvard University. Peter Chalk, a political scientist at RAND, is an expert on international terrorism and emerging global threats.

Several trends in modern society are exacerbating the incidence and spread of infectious disease. Foremost among these is the globalization of human interaction. The volume and speed of international travel inevitably hastens global transmission of disease. Around the world, people are increasingly relocating to mushrooming urban centers with inadequate sanitation and high population density, where disease spreads rapidly; meanwhile, commercial development and settlement in new habitats puts people in contact with previously unknown pathogens against which they have no immunity. Also, global warming is expanding the regions in which disease-causing organisms thrive.

The bubonic plague that swept across Europe during the Middle Ages, the smallpox that was carried to the Americas by the Spanish, and the influenza outbreak of 1918 all bear testimony to the historic relevance of infectious pathogens and their ability to cause widespread death and suffering. In many ways, however, the nature and magnitude of the threat posed by infectious pathogens are greater today than they have ever been in the past, developments in modern science notwithstanding. Emerging and reemerging infections present daily challenges to existing medical capabilities. Not only have deadly and previously unimagined illnesses, such as AIDS, Ebola, Creutzfeldt-Jakob disease, and Legionnaires' disease, emerged in recent years, but established diseases that just a few decades ago were thought to have been tamed are also returning, many in virulent, drug-resistant varieties. Modern manifestations of TB, for instance, bear little resemblance to the 19th-century strains that haunted Europe. TB treatment now requires a daily drug regimen that often requires health workers to personally monitor patients to ensure that they are complying with necessary procedures.

In many ways, this situation is a result of the natural balance of forces between people and infectious organisms. By one estimate, there are at least 5,000 kinds of viruses and more than 300,000 species of bacteria that challenge human beings, many of which are able to replicate and evolve billions of times in one human generation. These disparities clearly work to the advantage of pathogens, enabling the evolution of ever more virulent strains that quickly outstrip the ability of humans to respond to them. Just as important, however, are "artificial" disease force-multipliers, which are serving to greatly exacerbate the incidence and spread of infectious microbes. Foremost among these are globalization, modern medical practices, accelerating urbanization, climatic change resulting from global warming, and changing social and behavioral patterns. . . .

Globalization

The present international system is now more globally interdependent than at any other time in history. Today one can physically move from one part of the world to another in the same time (if not more rapidly than) it used to take to journey between cities or counties. Indeed, no part of the planet remains inaccessible to human penetration, with current estimates of the number of people crossing international frontiers on board commercial flights at more than 500 million every year. . . .

Whether measured on the basis of information flows, the total volume of world trade and commerce, contact between governments, or links between people, the figures all show major increases, especially over the last 20 years. While it is not necessary to spell out these developments in terms of specific statistics—the trends are both clear and well known—the consequences for the spread and emergence of infectious diseases do require some elucidation.

> *The speed of modern air transportation has greatly facilitated the global transmission of disease among humans.*

On one level, the global trade in agricultural products has increasingly brought people into contact with exotic and foreign animal diseases that have subsequently "jumped" across the species line to infect humans. Several examples stand out. In September 2000 a major outbreak of Rift Valley fever hit Saudi Arabia, killing several dozen people in a matter of days. The source of the epidemic was eventually traced back to imports of infected sheep from neighboring Yemen. In Europe, the emergence of the nervous system disorder Creutzfeldt-Jakob disease has been linked to the consumption of beef products originally derived from British cattle afflicted with bovine spongiform encephalopathy, or "Mad Cow Disease."

And in the United States, the outbreak of West Nile virus in 2000 is now believed to have originated at least partly from the importation of chickens into New York.

On a more direct level, the speed of modern air transportation has greatly facilitated the global transmission of disease among humans. Travelers experiencing either fully developed or incubating endemic or emerging diseases from their departure location can rapidly carry microbes into nonendemic areas. In the United Kingdom and the United States, for instance, there have been numerous cases of people living near major metropolitan airports contracting malaria apparently imported aboard jets operating transcontinental routes. Equally as indicative is typhoid fever. Roughly 400 cases of the disease are reported every year in America, 70 percent of which are acquired by individuals while traveling overseas. Outbreaks of Legionnaires' disease have been similarly linked to such dynamics. . . .

Compounding the problem is the fact that overcrowded, poorly ventilated, and (sometimes) unsanitary aircraft constitute ideal environments for the transmission of viruses and bacteria, particularly on long flights. Reflecting this, travel health guidelines issued by the World Health Organization (WHO) now specifically refer to the possibility of catching infectious TB in flight as "realistic," especially on flights of more than eight hours. The WHO has recorded several instances in which individuals flying on planes with other TB-infected travelers have been infected with the bacterium that causes the lung infection.

Improved medical practices have extended the lives of many ill people whose immune systems are less capable of combating microorganisms.

One disease that has certainly reached pandemic proportions at least partly as a result of globalization and the international movement of goods and people is AIDS. Studies in Africa have tracked the progress of the causative HIV agent along trucking routes, with major roads acting as principal corridors of viral spread between urban areas and other proximal settlements. In one study of 68 truck drivers and their assistants, 35 percent were found to be HIV-positive. Further epidemiological research revealed a wide travel history for these individuals, involving seven different countries served by the ports of Mombassa, including Kenya, Uganda, Zaire, Burundi, and Rwanda. Tourism, especially tourism involving sex, has also played a contributing role. There can be little doubt that the global spread of AIDS has been encouraged by the substantial patronage of the Asian sex markets and by the equally large number of international travelers visiting such countries as Thailand, India, and the Philippines every year.

Modern medical practices

During the 1960s and 1970s, there was a great deal of hope that humankind had tackled some of its worst infectious diseases through medical advances. This sense of confidence culminated in 1978 when the member states of the United Nations (UN) signed the Health for All, 2000, agreement. The accord set out ambitious goals for responding to infectious diseases among other things, predicting that at least some of the world's poorest and least developed states would undergo a fundamental (positive) health transition before the end of the century.

The optimism inherent in the UN declaration rested on the belief that advances in antibiotics, vaccines, and other remedial treatments—together with striking improvements in food preparation and water treatment—had provided the world's politics with a formidable armory that could be brought to bear against microbial agents. Indeed, just the year before, the WHO had announced the effective eradication of the smallpox virus after the last known case of smallpox had been tracked down and cured in Ethiopia.

While scientific progress has certainly helped to mitigate the effects of certain infectious ailments, overuse and misuse of antibiotics—both in humans and in the agricultural produce they consume—has contributed to a process of "pathogenic natural selection," which is helping to generate ever more resilient, resistant, and powerful disease strains. Much of this evolution stems from the rapidity with which microbes are able to adapt and replicate plasmid in their DNA and RNA codes, the genetic dynamic of which commands mutation under stress. Individuals who fail to complete prescribed treatment courses further aggravate the problem by allowing a residual, more resistant viral or bacterial base to survive and flourish. . . .

Modern medical science and/or associated practices are helping to heighten human vulnerability to viral and bacterial pathogens in other ways. Invasive treatment procedures are exposing people to hospital-acquired infections, including the [highly resistant] *S. aureus* bacterium. . . . This is particularly true in the developing world, where typically only the sickest—and, therefore, the most vulnerable—are hospitalized. The use of contaminated blood to make clotting agents and antibody plasma proteins such as gamma globulin has similarly exposed patients to highly debilitating diseases such as AIDS and hepatitis C—a problem becoming especially prevalent in China, where there exists a thriving illegal trade in blood.

Expanding metropolitan hubs are proving to be excellent breeding grounds for the growth and spread of infectious bioorganisms.

Just as serious are the nature and direction of contemporary medical research, which is exhibiting an increased predilection toward the wholesale eradication (rather than control) of microbial organisms. Significantly, much of this exploratory work is proceeding in the absence of a definitive understanding of the etiology of diseases and the environmental contexts in which they exist. As Joshua Lederberg, a Nobel prize–winning biologist, points out, this is liable to prove a highly costly (and misplaced) "war of attrition" in that it will probably merely upset the delicate ecological balance between microbes and their human hosts and, in so doing, exacerbate overall individual vulnerability to pathogenic infections and mutations.

Further, improved medical practices have extended the lives of many ill people whose immune systems are less capable of combating microorganisms. An increasing number of individuals in the United States and elsewhere are living with HIV/AIDS infection, cancer, transplanted organs, and aged immune systems. The presence of these people raises the likelihood that opportunistic pathogens will take hold.

Accelerating urbanization

At the turn of the 20th century, only 5 percent of the globe's inhabitants lived in cities with populations over 100,000. By the mid-1990s, more than 2.5 billion people resided in metropolitan centers. Most of this urban growth has taken place in the poorer parts of the world. In 1950, for instance, roughly 18 percent of the population of developing states lived in cities. By 2000, the number had jumped to 40 percent, and by 2030 it is expected to reach 56 percent. Several of these conglomerations will have populations in excess of ten million inhabitants. Indeed, according to the UN, 24 so-called "megacities" have already surpassed this demographic threshold, including Jakarta, Calcutta, Lagos, Karachi, and Mexico City.

Rapid intrusion into new habitats has disturbed previously untouched life forms and brought humans into contact with pathogens and contaminants for which they have little, if any, tolerance.

The reasons for the high rate of rural-urban migration throughout the developing world are complex and varied. However, they typically incorporate factors such as drought, flooding, and other natural disasters; an excess of agricultural labor; sociopolitical unrest generated by civil war; a lack of employment opportunities; and rural banditry. Fleeing these types of conditions (or variations of them), millions of dispossessed workers have moved to squalid shantytowns on the outskirts of major third-world cities, swelling urban populations and overloading already inadequate water, sanitary, medical, food, housing, and other vital infrastructural services. These expanding metropolitan hubs are proving to be excellent breeding grounds for the growth and spread of infectious bioorganisms. According to one study, a lack of clean water, sanitation, and hygiene alone account for an estimated 7 percent of all disease-related deaths that occur globally.

Asia in particular has been severely hit by the negative interaction between unsustainable city growth and disease spread. The region's urban population is currently estimated to be 1.1 billion. By 2025, it is expected to have risen to 3.8 billion and Asia will contain half the world's people—more than half of whom will live in cities. Nine of the aforementioned "megacities" already exist in the region, including Beijing, Calcutta, Jakarta, Mumbai (formerly Bombay), Osaka, Shanghai, Tianjin, and Tokyo. . . .

The infectious consequences of these developments are inevitable, with widespread outbreaks of typhoid, malaria, dengue fever, dysentery, and cholera a common occurrence. As [social critic and science writer] Eugene Linden observes:

> Advances in sanitation and the discovery of antibiotics have given humanity a respite from the ravages of infectious disease. But many epidemiologists [now] fear that this period is drawing to a close as urban growth outruns the installation of sanitation in the developing world and resilient microbes discover opportunities in the stressed immune systems of the urban poor.

Unsustainable urbanization can affect the spread of disease in other ways. Rapid intrusion into new habitats has disturbed previously untouched life forms and brought humans into contact with pathogens and contaminants for which they have little, if any, tolerance. Mushrooming cities in the developing world are also helping to transform oceans into breeding grounds for microorganisms. Epidemiologists have warned, for instance, that toxic algal blooms, fed by sewage, fertilizers, and other industrial and human contaminants from coastal metropolises in Asia, Africa, and Latin America contain countless viruses and bacteria. Mixed together in what amounts to a dirty "genetic soup," these pathogens can undergo countless changes, mutating into new, highly virulent antibiotic strains that can be quickly diffused by nautical traffic. The devastating cholera epidemic that broke out in Latin America in 1991, for instance, occurred after a ship from Asia unloaded contaminated ballast water into the harbor of Callao, Peru. The epidemic, which originated from a resistant strain of the El Tor serogroup, subsequently spread to neighboring countries, infecting more than 320,000 people and killing 2,600.

Environmental factors

Over the past century, humanity has dramatically affected the global biosphere in deep and complex ways. One important effect of such actions has been a gradual increase in the earth's average surface temperature, a change that many scientists now believe has the potential to actively contribute to the transnational spread of disease. According to two 2001 UN studies by the Intergovernmental Panel on Climate Change, the earth's temperature could rise between 1.4 and 5.8 degrees Celsius over the 1990 average surface temperature during the next century.

Global warming could expose millions of people for the first time to malaria, sleeping sickness, dengue fever, yellow fever, and other insect-borne illnesses.

Global warming could expose millions of people for the first time to malaria, sleeping sickness, dengue fever, yellow fever, and other insect-borne illnesses. In the United States, for instance, a slight increase in overall temperature would allow the mosquitoes that carry dengue fever to survive as far north as New York City. Also, the insects that carry the *Plas-*

modium falciparum parasite, which causes malaria, thrive in the warm climates of the tropics. Increased temperatures in more temperate areas could, conceivably, provide a habitat suitable for the increased distribution of these anopheline vectors. . . .

Global warming and climatic change may also influence the spread of disease by potentially increasing the incidence and magnitude of natural disasters such as landslides, storms, hurricanes, and flooding. Just as in war and conflict, these events invariably lead to the destruction/disruption of vital communication, health, and sanitation infrastructure as well as the displacement of people into overcrowded, makeshift shelters and camps. Such consequences are likely to have direct adverse effects on public health, transforming a disaster area into a potential "epidemiological time bomb." . . .

Changes in social and behavioral patterns

Changes in human social and behavioral patterns have had a profound impact on the spread of infectious illnesses. HIV/AIDS represents a case in point. Although the precise ancestry of HIV is uncertain, early transmission of the disease was undoubtedly facilitated by greater acceptance of multiple sexual partners and permissive homosexuality, particularly in nations such as the United States. Today, almost 1.4 million people are living with HIV throughout North America and Western Europe, with some cities, such as New York, among the places in the world where the disease is most prevalent. While the rate of new infections in the developed world slowed during the 1990s (especially in the United States)—largely because of the initiation of effective sex education campaigns and the availability of effective antiretroviral drugs—the disease continues to decimate Africa and South/Southeast Asia. Sub-Saharan Africa has been particularly badly affected, where a staggering 21.8 million people have died since the disease was first diagnosed in the early 1980s. Overall, the subcontinent accounts for roughly 70 percent of the world's AIDS cases and three-quarters of its AIDS-related deaths.

In Thailand, Cambodia, and India, thriving sex industries have served to compound already serious problems stemming from greater sexual promiscuity. More than 100,000 cases of AIDS were reported in Thailand between 1994 and 1998. Although an intensive campaign initiated by the government has helped to slow the overall rate of new infections in major centers such as Bangkok, the disease remains a serious problem in northern cities such as Chiang Rai, where roughly 40 percent of female prostitutes are thought to be HIV positive. In Cambodia, nearly half of *all* the country's sex workers are known to be infected by HIV, which causes AIDS. Based on current trends, a staggering 10 percent of the country's population could be infected by 2010. Figures for India are equally as serious. In Mumbai alone, 75 percent of the city's 60,000 to 70,000 prostitutes have contracted the disease, up from just 1 percent in 1990. In total, roughly 3.5 million people are currently thought to be living with the disease in India, a rate of infection that owes much to commercial sex and the high levels of sexually transmitted diseases (STDs) in the country. . . .

The increasing prevalence of intravenous drug use has also been instrumental in encouraging the spread HIV/AIDS. Burma, for example, which sits at the heart of the infamous opium-producing "Golden Triangle" and was free of HIV only a few years ago, now has an estimated 200,000 people carrying the virus, 74 percent of whom are intravenous drug users. Equally indicative is India, where intravenous drug use is now the second most common method of transmission for the disease (behind heterosexual sex), something that is especially true in the northeast regions that border Burma. China has been especially hard hit. The Beijing government freely admits that the outbreak of an AIDS epidemic in the country's south is directly related to drug addicts sharing needles to inject heroin. . . .

The development of large-scale factory farms and increased interactions between rural and urban populations have been linked to . . . the general increased incidence of zoonotic diseases that are passed from livestock to humans.

Although HIV/AIDS is the clearest example of how altered social and behavioral patterns have affected the occurrence and spread of infectious disease, it is not the only one. Changes in land use have also played a significant role. The emergence of Lyme disease in North America and Europe has been linked to reforestation and subsequent increases in the deer tick population, while conversion of grasslands to farming in Asia is believed to have encouraged the growth of rodents carrying hemorrhagic fever and other viral infections. In the United States and United Kingdom, the development of large-scale factory farms and increased interactions between rural and urban populations have been linked to outbreaks of *Salmonella* and cryptosporidiosis as well as the general increased incidence of zoonotic diseases that are passed from livestock to humans.

Finally, as society has moved into habitats requiring environmental modification, niches have been inadvertently created that are proving to be highly conducive for microbial growth and development. Heating and ventilation systems using water cooling processes, for instance, are now known to provide the perfect breeding ground and dissemination pathway for *Legionella pneumophila*, the causative agent of Legionnaires' disease.

Medical science has come a long way in improving our basic understanding of the origin and effect of most infectious diseases humans may contract. Nevertheless, we have proven far less adept at recognizing and effectively dealing with the factors that facilitate the spread of viral and bacterial agents. Through such things as urbanization, climatic change, changing social and behavioral patterns, globalization, and misappropriate/misguided remedial procedures, humanity is rapidly approaching what one commentator has referred to as the "twilight of the antibiotic era." Not only are we having trouble controlling age-old problems like TB, cholera, and malaria, but new, previously unimagined illnesses and viruses such as HIV/AIDS have emerged with a vengeance.

3

Bioterrorism Poses a Major Threat to Public Health

Mark G. Kortepeter and Gerald W. Parker

Mark G. Kortepeter is a preventive medicine officer in the Operational Medicine Division at the U.S. Army Medical Research Institute of Infectious Diseases (USAMRIID), where he teaches the medical management of biological weapons casualties. Gerald W. Parker is commander of the USAMRIID research facility, located in Fort Detrick, Maryland.

Bioterrorism poses a significant public health threat. A biological weapons attack could come from three main sources: well-funded and possibly state-supported large organizations, which aim to inflict mass casualties and are likely to conduct their own weapons production programs; smaller, less sophisticated groups, which are more likely to use accessible biological agents to publicize a cause; and individuals or very small groups using pathogens in murder plots or to threaten havoc. Approximately thirty-nine pathogens—including bacteria, viruses, and other toxins—are potential biological agents. However, certain criteria—primarily speed of contagion, environmental stability, ease of large-scale production, and toxicity or disease severity—suggest which of these agents have a high probability of use. Based on these factors, anthrax and smallpox pose the greatest risk.

The list of agents that could pose the greatest public health risk in the event of a bioterrorist attack is short. However, although short, the list includes agents that, if acquired and properly disseminated, could cause a difficult public health challenge in terms of our ability to limit the numbers of casualties and control the damage to our cities and nation.

The use of biological weapons has occurred sporadically for centuries, culminating in sophisticated research and testing programs run by several countries. Biological weapons proliferation is a serious problem that is increasing the probability of a serious bioterrorism incident. The accidental release of anthrax from a military testing facility in the former Soviet Union in 1979 and Iraq's admission in 1995 to having quantities of an-

Mark G. Kortepeter and Gerald W. Parker, "Potential Biological Weapons Threats," *Emerging Infectious Diseases*, vol. 5, July/August 1999.

thrax, botulinum toxin, and aflatoxin ready to use as weapons have clearly shown that research in the offensive use of biological agents continued, despite the 1972 Biological Weapons Convention. Of the seven countries listed by the U.S. Department of State [in 1999] as sponsoring international terrorism [Libya, Syria, Iran, Iraq, Cuba, Sudan, and North Korea], at least five are suspected to have biological warfare programs. There is no evidence at this time, however, that any state has provided biological weapons expertise to a terrorist organization.

A wide range of potential perpetrators

A wide range of groups or individuals might use biological agents as instruments of terror. At the most dangerous end of the spectrum are large organizations that are well-funded and possibly state-supported. They would be expected to cause the greatest harm, because of their access to scientific expertise, biological agents, and most importantly, dissemination technology, including the capability to produce refined dry agent, deliverable in milled particles of the proper size for aerosol dissemination. The Aum Shinrikyo in Japan is an example of a well-financed organization that was attempting to develop biological weapons capability. However, they were not successful in their multiple attempts to release anthrax and botulinum toxin [between 1990 and 1995]. On this end of the spectrum, the list of biological agents available to cause mass casualties is small and would probably include one of the classic biological agents. The probability of occurrence is low; however, the consequences of a possible successful attack are serious.

The probability of occurrence is low; however, the consequences of a possible successful attack are serious.

Smaller, less sophisticated organizations may or may not have the intent to kill but may use biological pathogens to further their specific goals. The Rajhneeshees, who attempted to influence local elections in The Dalles, Oregon, by contaminating salad bars with *Salmonella typhimurium*, are an example. Rather than having a sophisticated research program, these organizations could use biological pathogens that are readily available.

The third type are smaller groups or individuals who may have very limited targets (e.g., individuals or buildings) and are using biological pathogens in murder plots or to threaten havoc. The [late 1990s] anthrax hoaxes are examples of this. Many biological agents could be used in such instances and the likelihood of their occurrence is high, but the public health consequences are low.

A wide range of infectious agents

There are many potential human biological pathogens. A North Atlantic Treaty Organization handbook dealing with biological warfare defense lists 39 agents, including bacteria, viruses, rickettsiae, and toxins, that could be used as biological weapons. Examining the relationship between aerosol infectivity and toxicity versus quantity of agent illustrates the requirements for producing equivalent effects and narrows the spectrum of possible agents that could be used to cause large numbers of casualities. For example, the amount of agent needed to cover a 100-km^2 area and cause 50% lethality is 8 metric tons for even a "highly toxic" toxin such as ricin versus only kilogram quantities of anthrax needed to achieve the same coverage. Thus, deploying an agent such as ricin over a wide area, although possible, becomes impractical from a logistics standpoint, even for a well-funded organization. The potential impact on a city can be estimated by looking at the effectiveness of an aerosol in producing downwind casualties. The World Health Organization [WHO] in 1970 modeled the results of a hypothetical dissemination of 50 kg of agent along a 2-km line upwind of a large population center. Anthrax and tularemia are predicted to cause the highest number of dead and incapacitated, as well as the greatest downwind spread.

[Low actual casualty] numbers should not give a false sense of security that mass lethality is not achievable by a determined terrorist group.

For further indication of which pathogens make effective biological weapons, one could look at the agents studied by the United States when it had an offensive biological weapons research program. Under that program, which was discontinued in 1969, the United States produced the following to fill munitions: *Bacillus anthracis*, botulinum toxin, *Francisella tularensis*, *Brucella suis*, Venezuelan equine encephalitis virus, staphylococcal enterotoxin B, and *Coxiella burnetti*. As a further indication of which pathogens have the requisite physical characteristics to make good biological weapons, one need only look next at the agents that former Soviet Union biological weapons experts considered likely candidates. The agents included smallpox, plague, anthrax, botulinum toxin, equine encephalitis viruses, tularemia, Q fever, Marburg, melioidosis, and typhus. Criteria such as infectivity and toxicity, environmental stability, ease of large-scale production, and disease severity were used in determining which agents had a high probability of use. Both the United States before 1969 and the former Soviet Union spent years determining which pathogens had strategic and tactical capability.

The National Defense University . . . compiled a study of more than 100 confirmed incidents of illicit use of biological agents during [the twentieth] century. Of the 100 incidents, 29 involved agent acquisition, and of the 29, 19 involved the actual nongovernmental use of an agent, and most were used for biocrimes, rather than for bioterrorism. In the context of this study, the distinguishing feature of bioterrorism is that it involves the use of "violence on behalf of a political, religious, ecologic, or other ideologic cause without reference to the moral or political justice of the cause." The balance of incidents involved an expressed interest, threat of use, or an attempt to acquire an agent. In the 1990s, incidents increased markedly, but most have been hoaxes. The pathogens involved present a wide spectrum, from those with little ability to cause disease or disability, such as *Ascaris suum*, to some of the familiar agents deemed most deadly, such as *B. anthracis*, ricin, plague, and botulinum toxins. . . . During this period, the number of known deaths is only 10, while the total number of casualties is 990. However, the numbers should not give a false sense of security that mass lethality is not achievable by a determined terrorist group. The sharp increase in biological threats, hoaxes, information, and Internet sources on this subject seen in recent years indicates a growing interest in the possible use of biological pathogens for nefarious means.

Most dangerous scenarios involve anthrax or smallpox

In general, the existing public health systems should be able to handle most attempts to release biological pathogens. A working group organized by the Johns Hopkins Center for Civilian Biodefense Studies recently looked at potential biological agents to decide which present the greatest risk for a maximum credible event from a public health perspective. A maximum credible event would be one that could cause large loss of life, in addition to disruption, panic, and overwhelming of the civilian health-care resources.

To be used for a maximum credible event, an agent must have some of the following properties: the agent should be highly lethal and easily produced in large quantities. Given that the aerosol route is the most likely for a large-scale attack, stability in aerosol and capability to be dispersed (17 μm to 5 μm particle size) are necessary. Additional attributes that make an agent even more dangerous include being communicable from person to person and having no treatment or vaccine.

The death rate for anthrax if untreated before onset of serious symptoms exceeds 80%.

When the potential agents are reviewed for these characteristics, anthrax and smallpox are the two with greatest potential for mass casualties and civil disruption. 1) Both are highly lethal: the death rate for anthrax if untreated before onset of serious symptoms exceeds 80%; 30% of unvaccinated patients infected with variola major could die. 2) Both are stable for transmission in aerosol and capable of large-scale production. Anthrax spores have been known to survive for decades under the right conditions. WHO was concerned that smallpox might be freeze-dried to retain virulence for prolonged periods. 3) Both have been developed as agents in state programs. Iraq has produced anthrax for use in Scud missiles and conducted research on camelpox virus, which is closely related to smallpox. A Soviet defector has reported that the former Soviet Union produced smallpox virus by the ton. 4) Use of either agent would have a devastating psychological effect on the target population, potentially causing widespread panic. This is in part due to the agents' well-demonstrated historical potential to cause large disease outbreaks. 5) Initial recognition of both diseases is likely to be delayed. For anthrax, this is secondary to the rare occurrence of inhalation anthrax. Only 11 cases of inhalation anthrax have been reported in the United States from 1945 to 1994, and recognition may be delayed until after antibiotic use would be beneficial. For smallpox, given that few U.S. physicians have any clinical experience with the disease, many could confuse it for more common diseases (e.g., varicella and bullous erythema multiforme) early on, allowing for second-generation spread. 6) Availability of vaccines for either disease is limited. Anthrax vaccine, licensed in 1970, has been used for persons at high risk for contact with this disease. The U.S. military has recently begun vaccinating the entire force; however, there is limited availability of the vaccine for use in the civilian population. Routine smallpox vaccination was discontinued in the United States in 1971. Recent estimates of the current number of doses in storage at CDC [Centers for Disease Control and Prevention] range from 5 to 7 million, but the viability of stored vaccine is no longer guaranteed.

We know that biological pathogens have been used for biological warfare and terrorism, and their potential for future use is a major concern.

Obtaining smallpox virus as opposed to other agents (e.g., anthrax, plague, and botulinum toxin) would be difficult, but if obtained and intentionally released, smallpox could cause a public health catastrophe because of its communicability. Even a single case could lead to 10 to 20 others. It is estimated that no more than 20% of the population has any immunity from prior vaccination. There is no acceptable treatment, and the communicability by aerosol requires negative-pressure isolation. Therefore, these limited isolation resources in medical facilities would be easily overwhelmed.

Anthrax can have a delayed onset, further leading to delays in recognition and treatment. In the outbreak of inhalation anthrax in Sverdlovsk in 1979, some patients became ill up to 6 weeks after the suspected release of anthrax spores. The current recommendation for prophylaxis of persons exposed to aerosolized anthrax is treatment with antibiotics for 8 weeks in the absence of vaccine or 4 weeks and until three doses of vaccine have been given. The amount of antibiotics required for postexposure prophylaxis of large populations could be enormous and could easily tax logistics capabilities for consequence management.

Other lethal infectious agents

Other bacterial agents capable of causing a maximum credible event include plague and tularemia. Plague, like smallpox and anthrax, can decimate a population (as in Europe in the Middle Ages). An outbreak of plague could easily cause great fear and hysteria in the target population (as in the 1994 outbreak in India), when hundreds of thousands were reported to have fled the city of Surat, various countries embargoed flights to and from India, and importation of Indian goods was restricted. Both plague and tularemia are potentially lethal without proper treatment;

however, the availability of effective treatment and prophylaxis may reduce possible damage to a population. Both are infectious at low doses. Pneumonic plague's person-to-person communicability and untreated case-fatality rate of at least twice that of tularemia make it more effective than tularemia as an agent to cause mass illness.

Other agents of concern include the botulinum toxins and viral hemorrhagic fevers. Once again, both are highly lethal. Botulinum toxin is a commonly cited threat, and Iraq has admitted to producing it. Since intensive care would be required in treating both illnesses and ventilator management is life-saving for botulinum, both would easily tax existing medical care facilities. However, botulinum toxin may be a less effective agent because of relatively lower stability in the environment and smaller geographic coverage than other agents demonstrated in modeling studies. Producing and dispensing large amounts are also difficult.

A number of different viruses can cause hemorrhagic fever. These include (but are not limited to) Lassa fever, from the Arenaviridae family; Rift Valley fever and Crimean Congo hemorrhagic fever, from the Bunyaviridae family; and Ebola hemorrhagic fever and Marburg disease, from the Filoviridae family. These organisms are potential biological agents because of their lethality, high infectivity by the aerosol route shown in animal models, and possibility for replication in tissue culture.

Preparing appropriate responses

In summary, we know that biological pathogens have been used for biological warfare and terrorism, and their potential for future use is a major concern. Therefore we must be prepared to respond appropriately if they are used again. The technology and intellectual capacity exist for a well-funded, highly motivated terrorist group to mount such an attack. Although the list of potential agents is long, only a handful of pathogens are thought to have the ability to cause a maximum credible event to paralyze a large city or region of the country, causing high numbers of deaths, wide-scale panic, and massive disruption of commerce. Diseases of antiquity (including anthrax, smallpox, and plague), notorious for causing large outbreaks, still head that list. In addition, other agents, such as botulinum toxin, hemorrhagic fever viruses, and tularemia, have potential to do the same. By focusing on a smaller list of these low-likelihood, but high-impact diseases, we can better prepare for potential intentional releases, and hope to mitigate their ultimate impact on our citizens.

Many other pathogens can cause illness and death, and the threat list will always be dynamic. We must, therefore, have the appropriate surveillance system and laboratory capability to identify other pathogens, and we must improve our public health and medical capabilities to respond to the short list of the most dangerous naturally occurring biological pathogens that could be used as bioterrorism weapons.

4

The Threat of Bioterrorism Has Been Exaggerated

Victor W. Sidel, Robert M. Gould, and Hillel W. Cohen

Victor W. Sidel is Distinguished University Professor of Social Medicine, Albert Einstein College of Medicine, Bronx, New York. Robert M. Gould is an associate pathologist at Santa Teresa Community Hospital in San Jose, California, and president-elect of Physicians for Social Responsibility, which advocates the elimination of all weapons of mass destruction. Hillel W. Cohen is assistant professor of epidemiology and social medicine at Albert Einstein College of Medicine.

The federal government's multibillion-dollar bioterrorism preparedness campaign exaggerates the threat of infectious disease spread by biological warfare. Most recent terrorist incidents involved explosives, not biological agents, and even the dissemination of anthrax spores through the mails in 2001 caused fewer than twenty cases of illness. In fact, biological weapons that could cause catastrophic casualties are extremely hard to obtain and even harder to deploy. Moreover, pouring money into antibioterrorism research facilities where dangerous pathogens are cultured and stored only increases the risk of accidental exposure or theft for terrorist purposes. Americans should not be persuaded to give up civil rights, including the right to confidential medical records and freedom from forced quarantine, by military, intelligence, and law enforcement agencies that play on public fears in combating an exaggerated threat.

The [terrorist] attacks of September 11, 2001, and the subsequent dissemination of anthrax spores through the mails have led to an intensified campaign for preparedness against bioterrorism in the United States. Proposals include increased funding for local and national public health infrastructure, including investment in lab modernization and improved systems of surveillance and communication, as well as intensive education of health personnel to be better able to manage appropriately the early presentation of bioterror-associated infectious disease. Budgets are slated to be increased to strengthen the ability of hazardous materials

Victor W. Sidel, Robert M. Gould, and Hillel W. Cohen, "Bioterrorism Preparedness: Cooptation of Public Health?" *Medicine and Global Survival*, vol. 7, 2002, pp. 82–89. Copyright © 2002 by International Physicians for the Prevention of Nuclear War. Reproduced by permission.

("hazmat") teams and other local responders to effectively deal with terrorist attacks and to promote the development of new anti-microbial
agents and vaccines to handle all conceivable outbreaks.

Efforts should clearly be made for primary prevention of violence in
any form and for secondary prevention and effective treatment when necessary. For example, sharply increased funding for public health infrastructures, which have been starved for funds for years, should be provided
at every level; effective surveillance for disease outbreaks, whatever their
origin, is essential; training for public health and medical personnel in
handling emergencies, whatever their cause, should be expanded, as
should access to public health and medical services, without financial or
other barriers. The population should be educated on ways to avoid and
respond to health problems of all types. Nevertheless, attempts to build
long term public health capacity on the basis of what may well be exaggerated bioterrorism threats, while uncritically partnering with military,
national security, and law enforcement agency-led preparedness strategies
and programs could ultimately undermine our ability to effectively employ primary prevention against significant health threats. Such threats include—but are not limited to—emerging and re-emerging infectious diseases, global climate change and pollution, and the use of weapons of
mass destruction of all sorts, including biological weapons.

> *The morbidity and mortality bioterrorism has caused
> has been very small compared to . . . the
> extraordinary level of concern engendered by
> bioterrorist acts or the threat of them.*

While our collective imagination has been seized by fear of bioterrorism, it is useful to remember that the weapons most frequently used in the
United States for violence designed to cause fear and panic and, thereby,
to force changes in attitudes and in policies—violence that has been
termed "terrorism"—are small arms and light weapons, incendiaries, and
explosives. In the most recent major acts of terrorism—the 1993 underground explosion that damaged the World Trade Center, the destruction
of the Federal Building in Oklahoma City, and the attacks on U.S. em-
bassies in Africa and on the USS *Cole* in Yemen—explosives were used. In
the September 11, 2001, attacks on the World Trade Center and on the
Pentagon, fuel-laden airliners were used as explosive devices. The term *terrorism* has also been used to describe the use of incendiary and detonation
bombs during World War II on civilian targets such as Guernica, Warsaw,
Rotterdam, London, Coventry, Dresden, Hamburg, Tokyo, and Osaka and
to describe the use of nuclear bombs on Hiroshima and Nagasaki.

Bioterrorism is rare and rarely successful

In contrast, examples of "bioterrorism"—the use of chemical or biological weapons for terrorism—have been rare. In Oregon, followers of the
Bhagwan Shree Rajneesh contaminated salad bars at 10 restaurants with
salmonella in 1984, resulting in 751 reported cases of gastrointestinal ill-

ness but no deaths. In Japan, followers of Shoko Asahara who were members of the Aum Shinrikyo cult used the nerve agent Sarin to kill seven people in a Tokyo suburb in 1994 and used it again in 1995 in the Tokyo subway system to kill 11 people and to affect several thousand. The Center for Non-proliferation Studies at the Monterey Institute of International Studies has identified 285 incidents throughout the world since 1976 in which chemical or biological weapons have been used, most with little harm to humans. The recent dissemination of anthrax spores in the U.S. is believed, at the time of publication, to have caused fewer than 20 cases of cutaneous and inhalation anthrax (including five deaths from inhalation anthrax). The dissemination of anthrax in these incidents, the source of which remains unknown, has also been termed an act of bioterrorism. Despicable as these acts are, the morbidity and mortality bioterrorism has caused has been very small compared to that produced by the use of other weapons and small compared to the extraordinary level of concern engendered by bioterrorist acts or the threat of them.

> *There is no known evidence that inhalation anthrax can be spread by person-to-person contact.*

Despite the rarity of bioterrorist incidents, multi-billion dollar programs have been underway over the past three years in the U.S.—well before the anthrax cases appeared in 2001—for "preparedness" against bioterrorism. Many public health organizations—including the Centers for Disease Control and Prevention (CDC), other units of the U.S. Public Health Service, and numerous county and state departments of public health—are engaged in these programs. Institutes to study bioterrorism have been established and schools of public health are being encouraged to set up core curricula on the topic. Hundreds of presentations have been given advocating anti-bioterrorism programs and a huge, coordinated program involving law enforcement and national security agencies has been undertaken, with enormous implications for public health and medical care services.

There has simultaneously been an extraordinary proliferation of articles in medical and public health journals in the U.S. calling for expansion of these programs. The articles have argued that acceptance by medical and public health facilities of governmental and other funds for bioterrorism preparedness, despite the extremely low probability of a bioterrorism event occurring, would be useful if an event were to occur and, even if it did not, would be useful to strengthen medical and public health infrastructures so they can respond effectively to other health emergences—a so called dual-use strategy.

Conversely, a much smaller number of articles in medical and public health journals have urged caution. The present authors and other critics of these initiatives have argued that while anti-bioterrorism funding may provide additional support for needed health programs, the organizing principles and priorities of biopreparedness programs can lead to an adverse politicalization of medical and public health decision making that conforms with national security directives while diverting attention from much more pressing and critical endemic global health problems. Anti-bioterrorism programs have proliferated on the basis of scant evidence, with little public debate or independent review, and without adequate consideration of the real nature of the threat and of the possible negative consequences of mandated responses. These potential problems include:

- exaggeration, in order to support military programs and national security-state agendas, of the threat of use and the consequences of use by terrorists of chemical and biological weapons;
- diversion of resources from other, much more urgently needed, public health services;
- use of ineffective or potentially dangerous preventive measures;
- the risks of commingling public health programs with military, intelligence, and law enforcement programs.

Exaggeration of the threat

Bioterrorism has been presented as a major threat to public health, often based on exaggerated or fictional accounts of what "could" happen. A typical example occurred in 1997, when Secretary of Defense William Cohen held up a five-pound bag of sugar on a national television broadcast and declared that if the sugar were anthrax organisms, they could kill half the population of Washington, DC. Presentations such as these are designed to capture attention but contribute little to reasonable assessments of risk. In addition, reports of the risks of specific weapons have at times been erroneous or alarmist. For example, a commentary in the [British medical journal] *Lancet* in 1998 suggested that inhalation anthrax was transmissible from an individual with the disease to others, although there is no known evidence that inhalation anthrax can be spread by person-to-person contact. [Since the mid-1990s] and continuing into the post–September 11 period, a number of expert analysts have contended that the catastrophic threat of chemical and biological terrorism has been greatly exaggerated.

> *The catastrophic threat of chemical and biological terrorism has been greatly exaggerated.*

In order to make a reasonable estimate of risk, it is useful to distinguish between very different types of potential incidents. The most frightening would be the use of chemical or biological agents in a manner that would cause huge devastation and up to millions of casualties. Biological and chemical weapons of the kind and amounts that could cause such catastrophic casualties, including smallpox, are extremely difficult to obtain and still harder to deploy. At present, only nation states with well developed military, scientific, and technical capacity would have the ability to carry out such an attack. Violation of the international treaties and conventions prohibiting chemical and biological weapons use would bring universal condemnation even from those who might otherwise sympathize with the initiating nation, which would also risk a devastating retaliatory attack.

Incidents on a smaller scale—similar to those that occurred in Japan or Oregon or to the dissemination of anthrax spores in the U.S.—might indeed be within the capabilities of organizations or individuals. But it would be difficult for terrorist organizations, in secret and without government support, to develop a capacity that only a limited number of nation states have had the resources to acquire. For example, Aum Shinrikyo, the well financed cult in Japan that released nerve agent in the Tokyo subway, had been unable, despite years of attempts, to develop a usable biological weapon. Furthermore, weaponization of chemical and biological agents is difficult and dangerous, and would-be weaponizers may be more likely to hurt themselves than to hurt others.

The anthrax incidents of 2001, in addition to causing human disease and death, cost a great deal of societal energy and resources. Emergency response teams were even more stressed by suspicion and by the proliferation of anthrax hoaxes, which had increased in incidence even before the dissemination of spores in the fall of 2001. The increased number of hoaxes does not, however, constitute evidence of increased risk of real incidents. They are rather evidence of increased risk of hoaxes. The costs in money and in disruption caused by suspicion and by hoaxes may be adverse outcomes of the campaign against bioterrorism, since the scare scenarios about alleged dangers of bioterrorism had given false reports a credibility they did not deserve and would not have received even a few years ago. . . .

Current plans for groups such as the National Academy of Sciences and the Monterey Institute to develop more objective measures of threat assessment may offer some promise of discrimination between realistic and hyped scenarios. For the full range of competing benefits and risks of various interventions to be rationally weighed, it will be critical for such projects to incorporate perspectives of primary prevention, including intensified action to strengthen the Biological Weapons Convention and to alleviate the global conditions that provide reservoirs for emerging and re-emerging infectious disease. In the event that new bioterrorist incidents take place, it is likely that proponents of massive investment in anti-bioterrorism will claim that even more investment should have been made in their projects. But this claim will fail to consider how expensive and ineffective preparedness programs have been and how those investments might have been used more effectively for alternative programs.

Public health resources are already stretched

Allocation of public funds for social well-being and for public health programs—which are essential to the health of the people of the United States and of the world—should not be a "zero sum game." If additional resources are needed in a rich nation such as the U.S., those resources should be allocated. In the real world, however, setting priorities for public resource allocation among many urgent needs is usually required. The funds so far allocated to anti-bioterrorism projects are small compared to the very large U.S. military budget, which was further expanded by the Bush Administration in the wake of the September 11 attacks. More to the point, they are also small compared to the desperately underfunded public health, and social welfare budgets of the U.S. and the world. Investment of these funds in programs to improve education, nutrition, housing, and other measures for disease prevention for the world's peoples is likely to be far more useful for prevention of bioterrorism and for public health.

Emergency maneuvers conducted by metropolitan areas throughout the country as part of bioterrorism preparedness have already stretched limited municipal resources dedicated to public health and welfare. For example, in California, where counties already are struggling from increased energy costs and a softening economy, bioterrorism preparedness could drain an additional $80 million from the coffers of those governments, which supply most of the social services used by poor people and others. The most effective way to reduce bioterrorism is to reduce poverty, hunger, violence, and stockpiles of weapons of mass destruction and to work for a world characterized by social justice, health, and peace. The belief that such a strategy would be successful seems utopian, but it is no more utopian than belief that current or even currently visualized U.S. anti-terrorism programs will provide effective protection against the consequences of use of potential chemical or biological weapons. . . .

Dangerous preventive measures

Another new and dangerous bioterrorism initiative is the expansion of research facilities that study potential biological and chemical warfare agents. Highly toxic agents, such as smallpox and ebola virus, can be stored and studied in these "Level IV" facilities. Until recently, such activities were known to have taken place at a CDC facility in Atlanta and at the U.S. Army's Fort Detrick in Maryland. Under the new program, the public was informed that Plum Island, a Department of Agriculture laboratory on the edge of the New York metropolitan area, is being "upgraded" to Level IV and an unknown number of other such facilities is being opened. These facilities, it has been announced, will study ways to defend against potential biological and chemical warfare agents, including possible attempts to genetically engineer new agents that might pose additional proliferation problems.

Pursuit of some so-called "defensive" or "preventive" measures may not only lead to a risk of accidents but may also lead directly or indirectly to biological terrorism.

Such facilities are not immune to accidents and leaks, either onsite or during the transport of pathogens. For example, a researcher at the U.S. Army Medical Research Institute of Infectious Diseases (USAMRID) developed a case of glanders, a disease considered to have biowarfare potential. The researcher spent considerable time in his community before the diagnosis was made. The report of the case in the *New England Journal of Medicine* and the editorial that accompanied it used the case to argue for additional anti-bioterrorism preparedness. A letter from the authors in response pointed out that the case was an example of the risks of anti-bioterrorism programs, not of bioterrorism. Worldwide experiences with presumably fail-safe facilities such as nuclear power plants should remind us that accidents can and do happen. More Level IV facilities will tend to increase the chance that an accident could occur, a possibility underscored by a 2001 Department of Energy (DOE) Inspector General's audit that indicated that DOE's "biological select agent activities lacked organization, coordination, and direction . . . resulting in the potential for greater risk to workers and possibly others from exposure to biologic select agents and select agent materials." The chance of an accident may be remote, but perhaps less remote than the threat against which these facilities are supposed to guard.

Finally, there is evidence that the source of the anthrax spores that were disseminated through the mail in the United States during the fall of 2001 may have originated from samples supplied by USAMRID to U.S. laboratories. Pursuit of some so-called "defensive" or "preventive" measures may not only lead to a risk of accidents but may also lead directly or indirectly to biological terrorism.

Risks of commingling public health with security programs

Once a bioterrorist incident has occurred, the cooperation of medical and public heath agencies and personnel with law enforcement agencies and personnel may be necessary and appropriate for a short term "tactical" response to the emergency. Long term "strategic" collaboration and commingling of medical and public health programs with military, intelligence, and law enforcement programs, however, might compromise the independence of public health professionals and agencies and subordinate their priorities to the priorities of the military, intelligence, and law enforcement agencies themselves. At a news conference on January 22, 1998, in which President [Bill] Clinton announced new initiatives to address bioterrorism, the U.S. Secretary of Health and Human Services stated: "This is the first time in American history in which the public health system has been integrated directly into the national security system." Given the well documented history of public health collaboration with Cold War programs, which included numerous clandestine experiments on an unsuspecting American populace, there is reason to be concerned about issues ranging from the erosion of scientific integrity and ethical standards through restrictions of basic civil liberties and free access to information and services necessary for medical care and public health. . . .

The potential weakening of confidentiality protection and of forcible incarceration of those suspected of spreading communicable disease, and the alliance of medicine and public health with police and other investigatory authorities, would increase the suspicions of the most dispossessed of our society—particularly poor, immigrant (both documented and undocumented) and non-white people—who view governmental agencies, particularly local and state police departments, with well grounded distrust. Suspicions have already been aroused by the studies conducted by the U.S. Public Health Service in Tuskegee from the 1930s to the 1950s on African-American men with syphilis who were denied treatment for it, for which the U.S. Government has apologized. The increasing subordination of public health planning to military and police direction that is already taking place under the anti-bioterrorist programs and those that are being proposed will compound these suspicions and endanger medical and public health outreach to vulnerable populations.

In the area of control of weaponry, it should be noted that in 1999 the U.S. announced its intention to reject the appeals from other nations and from the World Health Organization (WHO) to destroy its stock of smallpox virus and in July 2001 withdrew from international attempts to strengthen the 1972 Biological Weapons Convention (BWC) "in order to protect military and trade secrets." In September 2001 the *New York Times* published information that demonstrated that the DOD (Department of Defense) was conducting tests of methods for production of biological weapons and conducting biological tests that other nations and arms control experts could view as contravening the BWC and that could lead to a new biological weapons arms race. And in November the formal withdrawal by the United States from the BWC Review Conference in Geneva led to such division among the nations attending the conference that they suspended their work for a year without any action to strengthen BWC enforcement provisions. The proposals to spend billions of dollars for dubious and dangerous secondary prevention and treatment of the medical consequences of use of biological weapons while blocking international efforts for primary prevention of their production and use is a contradiction of good public health practice. . . .

In short, the folk wisdom "When you sup with the devil, use a long spoon," is worth heeding. Given the well documented history of abuses by U.S. military, intelligence, and law enforcement agencies in the name of "national security" and the political agendas of the current U.S. administration, no spoon may be long enough to protect public health and medicine from being tainted by current and future violations of public trust. Those in the public health and medical community who understand the compelling need to tell the truth about public health and medical issues and to eradicate the root causes of the milieu in which terrorism thrives need to oppose forcefully a militarist paradigm of preparedness that fosters a deception that a "Fortress America" free of microbial assaults can be achieved. If our nation is serious about preventing epidemics, from whatever causes, it must transcend its current "bunker mentality" and focus on the full range of primary prevention strategies, which include abolition of all weapons of mass destruction and include determined actions to achieve global health for all.

5

Bioterrorism Research Diverts Attention from More Serious Disease Threats

Merrill Goozner

Merrill Goozner, a contributing editor of the American Prospect *and professor of journalism at New York University, is the author of* The $800 Million Pill: Public Research, Private Profit, and the Truth About Pharmaceutical Innovation.

Since the September 11, 2001, terrorist attacks, federal funding for bioterrorism research has grown to become second only to funding for cancer research. Not surprisingly, in private and academic research labs across the country, medical researchers are following the grant money and phasing out basic research into the world's major infectious diseases—tuberculosis, malaria, and cholera, among others—in favor of studying rare pathogens that have been targeted as potential bioterrorism agents by the federal government. A better strategy would be to fund research into the infectious diseases that are ravaging the developing world; the results of those programs not only could be used to understand and develop vaccines against biological agents but would reduce widespread deprivation and misery—conditions that breed terrorists.

D r. Marcus Horwitz, professor of medicine at the University of California, Los Angeles, has devoted most of his career to finding a vaccine for tuberculosis. Though the age-old killer is well controlled in the industrialized world, TB kills more than 2 million people each year among the global poor. It's not a sexy field: Compared with funding for heart-disease, HIV/AIDS or cancer research, National Institutes of Health [NIH] money for TB research is a minor blip. Applied research into potential TB cures and vaccines is not a priority for the agency, or for drug companies, which see no profitable market among the poor. Still, after 15 years of research funded mainly by the NIH, Horwitz's lab has finally come up with what could be the first improvement in TB vaccination technology in nearly a

Merrill Goozner, "Bioterror Brain Drain: Infectious-Disease Specialists Are Following the Big Bucks to Washington's New Multibillion-Dollar Program on Bioterrorism Research—but at What Human Cost?" *American Prospect*, vol. 14, October 2003, pp. 30–33. Copyright © 2003 by The American Prospect, Inc., 5 Broad St., Boston, MA 02109. All rights reserved. Reproduced by permission.

century. His vaccine is being tested among a small group of patients, and a nonprofit drug development organization funded by the Bill and Melinda Gates Foundation is committed to sponsoring the full-blown efficacy trials if his early experiment proves successful.

So why, on the cusp of real progress, is Horwitz's lab phasing out its basic science research on TB in favor of studying tularemia, the bacterium spread by ticks and rodents that causes rabbit fever? Because tularemia is on the government's A-list of potential bioterrorism agents, put there because the United States and the former Soviet Union stockpiled it as a biological warfare agent during the Cold War. Today, Washington is throwing plenty of money at basic research of the pathogen even though it affects only a few hundred Americans a year, is relatively rare around the world and is easily treatable with common antibiotics. Even if it did fall into the hands of terrorists, the threat would hardly be grave: The disease is difficult to weaponize and, when treated, is fatal in fewer than 2 percent of cases. "Scientists call it money transferase," says Horwitz. In his case, the $200,000 he's received annually to study one of the globe's most virulent killers, TB, will now mainly go to study a disease whose significance is primarily symbolic in the war on terrorism.

Direct spending on bioterrorism research . . . [soared in 2003] to well over $2 billion. . . . By comparison, the NIH . . . spent less than $200 million on tuberculosis and malaria combined.

It's a scenario that's being played out across the country. Since the 2001 attacks, Congress has poured billions into bioterrorism research aimed at developing vaccines and drugs to combat the most likely threat agents. Indeed, the amount of money being directed at bioterrorism defense will soon make it the second-largest (after cancer) results-oriented medical research program of the post–Cold War era. And that has led the tiny fraternity of research scientists who've devoted their lives to studying infectious disease to expand or alter their research priorities in order to tap into the huge pot of money the government has set aside for bioterrorism research. Dr. Richard Guerrant, director of the Center for Global Health at the University of Virginia, for example, has tailored a few of his grants to win biodefense funding. "[Y]ou adopt what you do to attract the resources that are necessary," he said, adding that several of his colleagues at the center have shifted their "whole approach to tularemia and anthrax because of the availability of funding."

Skyrocketing bioterrorism budgets

The drive to protect the nation against potential bioterrorism agents is having a major impact on the entire medical-research establishment. Direct spending on bioterrorism research and development by the National Institute of Allergy and Infectious Diseases (the lead NIH agency in bioterrorism defense research) and the Department of Defense soared from an annual $250 million pre-anthrax attacks to well over $2 billion [in 2003], turning it almost overnight into a larger program than HIV/AIDS was in its heyday. By comparison, the NIH [in 2002] spent less than $200 million on tuberculosis and malaria combined. Meanwhile, the rest of the nation's medical-research budget is facing its first restrictive environment in decades. The NIH's overall research budget will rise only at the rate of inflation [in 2004]—far below the double-digit increases of the Clinton years. The belt-tightening prompted virtually every medical school and patient advocacy group in the country to sign full-page ads in the *Washington Post* last summer protesting the situation.

The actual development of candidate drugs and vaccines for potential bioterrorism agents . . . would have little effect on the diseases that pose the gravest threat to humankind.

Meanwhile, Congress upped the ante [in 2003] by quietly approving President George W. Bush's Project BioShield, a $5.6 billion fund to purchase the fruits of biodefense research. . . .

The idea behind BioShield is to entice for-profit pharmaceutical and biotech firms to invest in antiterrorism therapeutics, as they've made it plain that they won't ride to the nation's rescue unless they're lured with a guaranteed payoff. Eli Lilly head Sidney Taurel, who . . . drew fire from liberals on Capitol Hill for pushing for drug-industry liability exemptions from his perch atop the Homeland Security Advisory Council, indecorously encapsulated the industry's attitude in his public testimony [in 2002]. "Government is not going to get new miracle drugs for cost plus 10 percent," he said. Unlike run-of-the-mill defense contractors, the very profitable drug companies appear to have better uses for their capital.

No guarantees bioterrorism research will pay off

Even with this pot of gold at the end of the research-and-development rainbow, the path to a payoff will be long and tortuous. The biggest problem is scientific. Finding antidotes to infectious disease isn't easy. It will take years, in some cases decades, to develop new or more effective vaccines and drugs to combat anthrax, botulism, smallpox, tularemia and the other pathogens on the government's list of agents likely to be weaponized by nations or groups hoping to wreak havoc on the United States. No wonder major pharmaceutical companies are reluctant to dive in. Why invest in risky biodefense products when there are more lucrative heartburn-, allergy-, and pain-relief markets to pursue? Republicans in Congress seemed to recognize the flaw in relying on the market to protect the public against bioterrorism. During the bill's markup, . . . they slipped in an amendment allowing the government to manufacture the drugs and vaccines directly if procuring them from private contractors proves too costly.

Another problem is that even if these drugs were developed quickly, the effectiveness of the new therapeutics would remain in doubt. Most antibioterrorism drugs would never get the extensive clinical trial testing usually demanded by the Food and Drug Administration because there is no naturally occurring patient population on which to test them. Special exemptions have been built into the laws that allow vaccines to gain approval with only limited safety testing. If the public's reluctance to line up for the smallpox vaccine is any guide, new biodefense vaccines would simply be put on the shelf for the day when a coordinated and large scale bioterrorist attack makes the public receptive to mass inoculation. For many antibioterrorism agents, their first use would also be their first clinical trial.

The number of people worldwide who suffer from smallpox, botulism, Ebola or anthrax . . . wouldn't fill up the tuberculosis ward in a small African city.

Furthermore, a lot of the basic research money pouring into biodefense would be wasted on poor quality research. It's an inevitable outcome of the NIH peer-review process. Those familiar with the process say the closed-door panels divide applications into three piles: those that will get funded, those that will get funded if there's enough money and those in the "no way" pile. The sudden influx of funding inevitably means "you're reaching applications with less scientific merit," says Richard Ebright, who directs the chemistry lab at the Waksman Institute of Microbiology at Rutgers University. "There will be an enormous increase of people moving into bioterrorism, particularly people who have difficulty getting their grants funded." A similar process is under way in the private sector. Small biotechnology companies running out of venture capital are abandoning other projects to apply to the NIH for the small-business components of the antibioterrorism program.

What about TB, malaria, and cholera?

Most disappointing of all, the majority of the applied research supported by the government—the actual development of candidate drugs and vaccines for potential bioterrorism agents—would have little effect on the diseases that pose the gravest threat to humankind. Dr. Anthony Fauci, director of the National Institute of Allergy and Infectious Diseases (NIAID) and a leading figure in the nation's biodefense effort, claims there will be many "spin-offs" from beefing up bioterrorism defense research. He argues on the agency's Web site that "NIAID research on organisms with bioterror potential will almost certainly lead to an enhanced understanding of other more common and naturally occurring infectious diseases that afflict people here and abroad," like TB and malaria. But enhanced understanding is not a cure. Vaccine research is almost always pathogen specific, as are most new drugs to combat viral diseases. And the number of people worldwide who suffer from smallpox, botulism, Ebola or anthrax in the absence of deliberate poisonings wouldn't fill up the tuberculosis ward in a small African city. "It's distracting from global health," said Dr. Carol Nacy, founder of the Sequella Global Tuberculosis Foundation (which will fund Horwitz's large-scale TB trial) and now head of a small biotech firm researching TB drugs. "We'll learn some things [from bioterrorism research] that are relevant, but not much."

So far, she seems to be right. Far from pursuing spinoff, many scientists are shifting their priorities to follow the money. Johnny Peterson, a professor of microbiology and immunology at the University of Texas Medical Branch in Galveston, has been studying cholera since his graduate-student days in the late 1960s. Periodic outbreaks of dehydrating diarrhoeal diseases like cholera and dysentery kill an estimated 2 million children around the world every year because their bodies are so severely weakened by a lack of fluids and undernourishment, according to the Population Resource Center. (While those numbers aren't relatively large, cholera is a serious problem because children who survive it almost always suffer long-term damage.) Peterson has spent decades looking for compounds that block the bacterium's toxin, which leads to diarrhea, dehydration and death, and he's come up with at least one. But [in 2002] he saw that the compound might also block the related anthrax toxin, so he applied for a grant to study that. "We're trying to make hay when the sun is out," Peterson said. While he's hiring more scientists and will continue studying the basic science of cholera, his plans to seek a grant to apply his work to potential cholera therapeutics have been put on hold. "Perhaps we can pursue it in the future," he said.

By joining the fight against the infectious diseases ravaging the developing world, the United States can help drain the swamp that breeds terrorists.

There will be some positive spinoffs from increased biodefense spending, to be sure. Money hopefully will get channeled into rebuilding the nation's network of public-health clinics, which were created to cope with the epidemics that ravaged Americas cities over a century ago. The [2003] SARS [severe acute respiratory syndrome, a previously unknown viral disease that has killed more than seven hundred people worldwide] outbreak reminded everyone of the importance of having an infrastructure able to rapidly diagnose and understand newly emerging diseases. There will also be a major hunt for new "broad spectrum" antibiotics—drugs that are effective against a range of bacterial diseases including those that actually infect large numbers of people. There will be new research tools developed that can be deployed in the hunt for cures or vaccines for any infectious disease. This is especially important in an era when older antibiotics are rapidly becoming ineffective due to resistance brought on by overprescription, improper use and the inevitable mutations of wily microbes.

Barriers to applying bioterrorism research to other diseases

But who will own these new antibiotics? And who will test them against diseases like multidrug resistant TB, a growing global threat? Unlike their use as antibioterrorism agents, these new drugs will have to be tested against each specific disease before regulators here or abroad allow them into widespread use. And the basic economics of who conducts such tests will not be changed by BioShield's purchasing of biodefense research: Only testing for use against potential terrorism agents will be funded; research into secondary uses will not. For their part, the biotechnology and pharmaceutical industries have not invested in developing drugs for the major infectious disease killers for the same reasons they under invest in rare diseases in the United States: there's no market. For diseases like malaria, leishmaniasis and cholera, the market's absence isn't defined by the small number of patients but by the fact that the millions of patients have no money. Testing a new antibiotic that is effective against anthrax to see if it is also effective against tuberculosis will require that it be tested against tuberculosis. And that will require money that no drug company wants to spend. It would be a terrible denouement for the spinoff promise if the new and untested anti-terrorism drugs get stockpiled in military warehouses while scientists who want to test them on sick populations can't because they don't have the rights or the money to conduct the tests.

One way to get around this problem would be for the government to earmark a good portion of the $2 billion–plus for antibioterrorism research—say, one-quarter of it—for targeted research and development toward new therapeutics to combat the great neglected diseases that kill millions each year. This will not detract from the war on bioterrorism; it will enhance it. How? Spinoff works in both directions. A new antibiotic that cures multidrug resistant TB may be just what we need for the day when a mad scientist-terrorist figures out a way to aerosolize tularemia over one of our cities. And unlike some new antibiotic developed with that remote bioterrorism threat in mind, the new antibiotic will have been tested in large clinical trials, so its side effects will be well characterized. And it's not only good science, it's good politics. As one scientist put it, by joining the fight against the infectious diseases ravaging the developing world, the United States can help drain the swamp that breeds terrorists. "[I]t is a very clear way to address ideologically the threat of bioterrorism," said Guerrant of the Center for Global Health. "If we can do something about diarrhea or malaria, that will affect my children's future security better than anything else we can do."

6

AIDS Is Devastating Africa

Karen A. Stanecki

Karen A. Stanecki is chief of the Health Studies Branch of the U.S. Bureau of the Census Center for International Research in Washington, D.C., and a senior adviser on demographic data for the Joint United Nations Programme on HIV/AIDS (UNAIDS) in Geneva, Switzerland.

Seventy percent of the world's HIV-positive individuals live in sub-Saharan Africa. The disastrous effects of HIV/AIDS on the African continent are unprecedented. By 2010, Botswana, Mozambique, Lesotho, South Africa, and Swaziland will be experiencing negative population growth due to AIDS mortality. Life expectancies are falling drastically across the continent, infant mortality is rising, and African governments that were unprepared for the deaths of 15 million Africans from AIDS between 1982 and 2002 are facing the grim prospect that 15 to 20 million more will die of AIDS before 2010.

Over 90 percent of the people infected with the Human Immunodeficiency Virus (HIV), which causes AIDS, live in the developing world. The Joint United Nations Programme on HIV/AIDS (UNAIDS) expects that this "proportion will continue to rise in countries where poverty, poor health systems, and limited resources for prevention and care fuel the spread of the virus."

An estimated 70 percent of the global total of HIV-positive people, 26 million out of 37.1 million, live in Sub-Saharan Africa. Sub-Saharan Africa contains only 11 percent of the global population. Nine percent of all adults in Sub-Saharan Africa are HIV positive compared to 0.6 percent of adults in the United States. Since the beginning of the epidemic, over 15 million Africans have died from AIDS; 2.2 million AIDS deaths occurred there in 2001.

Southern and eastern Africa have been the most severely affected regions. Seven countries have an estimated adult (15–49) HIV prevalence of 20 percent or greater: Botswana, Lesotho, Namibia, South Africa, Swaziland, Zambia, and Zimbabwe. In these countries, all in southern Africa, at least one adult in five is living with HIV. An additional 6 countries, Burkina Faso, Cameroon, Central African Republic, Kenya, Malawi and Mozambique,

Karen A. Stanecki, "The AIDS Pandemic in the 21st Century," draft report of the XIV International Conference on AIDS, Barcelona, July 2002, U.S. Agency for International Development, Bureau for Global Health, Office of HIV/AIDS.

have adult HIV prevalence levels higher than 10 percent.

The HIV/AIDS epidemics in southern Africa started later but they have been explosive, such as in Botswana, where HIV prevalence among pregnant women in Francistown increased from 7 percent in 1991 to 44 percent in 2000.

The two notable success stories in Sub-Saharan Africa continue to be Uganda and Senegal. HIV prevalence among pregnant women in Uganda continues to decline in most sentinel surveillance sites. In Kampala, HIV prevalence declined from its peak of 30 percent in 1993 to 11 percent in 2000. In Senegal, AIDS control programs have managed to keep HIV prevalence at very low levels. . . .

In Sub-Saharan Africa, more women than men are HIV positive

At the end of 1999, UNAIDs estimated that 55 percent of all HIV infections in Sub-Saharan Africa were among women. Peak HIV prevalence among women occurs at a younger age than among men. Among women, HIV prevalence tends to peak around 25 years of age. Peak HIV prevalence among men occurs 10–15 years later and generally at lower levels. . . . Younger women have higher levels of HIV infection than men of their same age cohort.

By the year 2010, five [African] countries will be experiencing negative population growth because of AIDS mortality.

Several studies comparing HIV prevalence among pregnant women attending antenatal clinics with HIV prevalence among adult men and women from community based studies have shown that HIV prevalence among pregnant women gives a reasonable overall estimate of HIV prevalence in the general adult population. HIV prevalence among pregnant women tends to underestimate the prevalence among all women but overestimate HIV prevalence among men.

Mortality patterns are driven by HIV prevalence patterns

Median survival with HIV/AIDS is estimated to be around 10 years. In South Africa, by 2020, mortality for adults ages 20–45 will be much higher than it would have been without AIDS. Mortality for women will peak during the ages of 30–34, earlier than the peak seen for men during the ages of 40–44.

At the beginning of the twenty-first century, the population growth rate in Botswana is less than zero due to AIDS mortality. Other countries with sharply reduced growth rates include several other southern African countries: Lesotho, Malawi, Namibia, South Africa, Swaziland, and Zimbabwe. . . .

By the year 2010, five countries will be experiencing negative popu-

Population by Age and Sex with and Without AIDS for South Africa: 2002, 2010, and 2020

Population structures of badly affected countries will be radically altered by HIV

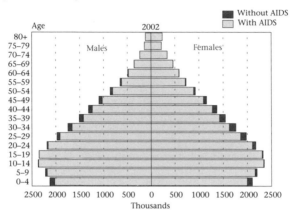

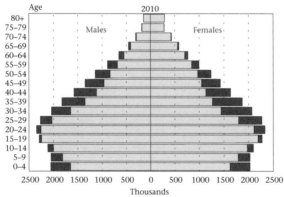

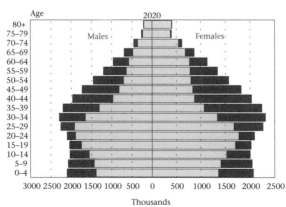

lation growth because of aids mortality. The growth rate for Botswana will continue to be suppressed and by 2010 it will be –2 percent. In South Africa it will be –1.4 percent and in Swaziland a –0.4 percent. [In Mozambique and Lesotho it will be –0.2 percent.] This negative population growth is due to the high levels of HIV prevalence in these countries and relatively low fertility. Previously, HIV/AIDS experts never expected HIV prevalence rates to reach such high levels for any country. By the end of 2001, adult HIV prevalence had reached an estimated 39 percent in Botswana, 20 percent in South Africa, and 33 percent in Swaziland. Zimbabwe and Namibia will be experiencing a growth rate of close to zero. Without AIDS, these countries would have been experiencing a growth rate of 2 percent or greater. . . .

In Botswana, life expectancy is now 39 instead of 72.

AIDS mortality will produce population pyramids that have never been seen before. Particularly in those countries with projected negative population growth, Botswana, Lesotho, Mozambique, South Africa, and Swaziland, population pyramids will have a new shape—"the population chimney." The implications of this new population structure are not clear. By 2020, between the ages of 15 and 44, there will be more men than women in each of the five-year-age cohorts, which may push men to seek partners in younger and younger age cohorts. This factor in turn may increase HIV infection rates among younger women. Current evidence indicates that older men are infecting younger women, who then go on to infect their partners, particularly through marriage. This vicious cycle could result in even higher HIV infection levels. . . .

AIDS mortality is resulting in falling life expectancies

Already, life expectancies have fallen in many countries in Sub-Saharan Africa from levels that would have been seen without AIDS. In Botswana, life expectancy is now 39 instead of 72. In Zimbabwe, life expectancy is 40 instead of 69. In fact, seven countries in Sub-Saharan Africa: Angola, Botswana, Lesotho, Malawi, Mozambique, Rwanda, and Zambia have life expectancies below 40 years of age. Each of the countries, except for Angola, would have had an estimated life expectancy of 50 years or greater without AIDS. . . .

In less than ten years time, many countries in southern Africa will see life expectancies fall to near 30 years of age, levels not seen since the end of the 19th century. In southern Africa, life expectancies will be falling to levels that have not been seen in over 100 years. In a region that would have expected life expectancies to reach 70 years of age by 2010, many will see life expectancies falling to around 30:

- Botswana—27 years
- Namibia—34 years
- Swaziland—33 years
- Zambia—34 years

Many other countries will see life expectancies falling to 30–40 years of age instead of 50–60 years. . . .

The most direct impact of AIDS is to increase the number of deaths in affected populations.

Crude death rates, the number of people dying per 1,000 population, have already been affected by AIDS.

In Africa, HIV epidemics have had their greatest impact in the eastern and the southern regions. Adult HIV prevalence is 20 percent or higher in seven countries and an additional six countries have HIV prevalence rates between 10 percent and 20 percent. In many of these countries, reports indicate the presence of the HIV virus since the early 1980s.

As a result of these high levels of HIV infection over several years, estimated crude death rates including AIDS mortality are greater by 50–500 percent in eastern and southern Africa over what they would have been without AIDS. For example, in Kenya with an adult HIV prevalence of 15 percent at the end of 2001, the crude death rate is estimated to be more than twice as high, 15.7, as it would have been without AIDS, 6.2. In South Africa, with an estimated 20 percent adult HIV prevalence level, the crude death rate is also twice as high, 16.6, as it would have been without AIDS, 7.3. . . .

Infant mortality rates are now higher than they were in 1990

AIDS mortality has reversed the declines in infant mortality rates that had been occurring during the 1980s and early 1990s. Over 30 percent of all children born to HIV infected mothers in Sub-Saharan Africa will be HIV positive either through the birth process or due to breast feeding. The relative impact of AIDS on infant mortality rates, the number of infants who will die before their first birthday out of 1000 live births, will depend on both the levels of HIV prevalence in the population and the infant mortality rate from other causes. In 1990 the infant mortality rate in Zimbabwe was 52; in 2002 it is 66. In South Africa, the infant mortality rate in 1990 was 51, in 2002 it is 60. Without AIDS, infant mortality in Zimbabwe and South Africa would likely have been 35 and 39, respectively.

The current burden of disease, death, and orphanhood will be a significant problem in many countries of Sub-Saharan Africa for the foreseeable future.

In countries with less severe epidemics, such as in western and central Africa, infant mortality rates are still higher than they would have been without AIDS. The increase ranges from 3 percent in Benin to 13 percent in Côte d'Ivoire and in Rwanda. . . .

In four countries of Sub-Saharan Africa, more infants will die from AIDS in 2010 than from all other causes. In Botswana and Zimbabwe, twice as many infants will die from AIDS as from all other causes. South Africa and Namibia are the other two countries where more infants will die from AIDS than from all other causes. Although overall infant mortality rates are projected to decline between 2000 and 2010, infant mortality due to AIDS is projected to increase. . . .

At the beginning of the 21st century, AIDS is the number one cause of death in Africa and fourth globally

Emerging just 20 years ago, few would have predicted the current state of the epidemic, particularly in Sub-Saharan Africa. That over 30 percent of adults would be living with HIV/AIDS in any country was unthinkable. Yet, this is the current situation in four countries. In seven Sub-Saharan African countries, at least one out of five adults are living with HIV/AIDS and in an additional six Sub-Saharan African countries, one out of ten adults is HIV positive.

Many individuals and governments have difficulty grasping the reality of these high prevalence levels. The resulting AIDS mortality is difficult to comprehend. Yet given these current rates, many more millions of individuals will die due to AIDS over the next decade than have over the past two decades. Many of the southern African countries are only beginning to see the impact of these high levels of HIV prevalence.

There have been success stories: . . . In . . . Uganda, concerted efforts at all levels of civil society have turned around increasing HIV prevalence rates. In Senegal, programs put into place early in the epidemic have kept HIV prevalence rates low. These successes can be repeated. However, the current burden of disease, death, and orphanhood will be a significant problem in many countries of Sub-Saharan Africa for the foreseeable future.

7

AIDS Is Not the Cause of the African Health Crisis

Charles Geshekter

Charles Geshekter is a professor of African history at California State University at Chico. He is one of several AIDS dissidents—a group of scientists and researchers who argue that HIV is a harmless virus and that toxic HIV medications such as AZT actually cause AIDS—appointed to the AIDS Advisory Panel convened by South African president Thabo Mbeki in June 2000.

Dire warnings that AIDS is causing an infectious disease crisis in Africa cannot be supported with hard data. In Africa AIDS is defined as a combination of symptoms that cannot be distinguished from the classic indigenous sicknesses of impoverished regions, such as tuberculosis and malaria. In fact, no HIV test is required for a positive diagnosis of AIDS. Alarming estimates of African AIDS deaths in the Western media are grossly at odds with the World Health Organization's much lower figures. Instead of stigmatizing Africans as sexually promiscuous and encouraging condom use to prevent AIDS, AIDS activists should focus on improving nutrition, water supplies, and sanitation, the underlying causes of the real health problems in Africa.

The United Nations calls AIDS the "worst infectious disease catastrophe since bubonic plague." U.S. Senator Barbara Boxer advocates spending $3 billion to "fight" the alleged culprit, HIV. And delegates at [the February 2000] National Summit on Africa in Washington, D.C., pleaded for more money to wage war on AIDS, by which they also mean HIV. But the scientific data do not support the view that what is being called AIDS in Africa has a viral cause. . . .

Let's start with a few basic facts about HIV, AIDS, African record-keeping and socio-economic realities. What are we counting? The World Health Organization defines an AIDS case in Africa as a combination of fever, persistent cough, diarrhea, and a 10 percent loss of body weight in two months. No HIV test is needed. It is impossible to distinguish these common symptoms—all of which I've had while working in Somalia—

from those of malaria, tuberculosis, or the indigenous disease of impover-ished lands. By contrast, in North America and Europe, AIDS is defined as 30-odd diseases occurring in people who test "HIV-positive." The lack of any requirement for such a test in Africa means that, in practice, many tra-ditional African diseases can be and are reclassified as AIDS. Since 1994, tu-berculosis itself has been considered an AIDS indicator disease in Africa.

The scientific data do not support the view that what is being called AIDS in Africa has a viral cause.

Dressed up as HIV/AIDS, a variety of old sicknesses have been reclas-sified. Post mortems are seldom performed in Africa to determine the ac-tual cause of death. According to the Global Burden of Disease Study, Africa maintains the lowest levels of reliable vital statistics for any conti-nent—a microscopic 1.1 per cent. "Verbal autopsies" are widely used be-cause death certificates are rarely issued. When AIDS experts are asked to prove actual cases of AIDS, terrifying numbers dissolve into vague esti-mates of HIV infection.

Unreliable record-keeping

The most reliable statistics on AIDS in Africa are found in the [World Health Organization] WHO Weekly Epidemiological Record. The total cu-mulative number of AIDS cases reposed in Africa since 1982, when AIDS record-keeping began, is 794,444—a number starkly at odds with the lat-est scare figures, which claim 2.3 million AIDS deaths throughout Africa for 1999 alone.

More reliable, locally based statistics rarely exist. In December [1999], I interviewed Alan Whiteside of the University of Natal, a top AIDS re-searcher in South Africa, and asked for details of the alleged 100,000 AIDS deaths in South Africa [that] year. He laughed aloud. "We don't keep any of those statistics in this country," he said. "They don't exist."

And South Africa is more advanced than most African countries in that it conducts HIV tests in surveys of about 18,000 pregnant Africans annually. The HIV-positive numbers are then extrapolated. But there are two problems with this: The women are given a blood test known as ELISA, which frequently gives a "false positive" result (one condition that can trigger a false alarm is pregnancy). Even the packet insert in the ELISA test kit from Abbott Labs contains the disclaimer: "There is no recognized standard for establishing the presence or absence of HIV-1 antibody in human blood."

Other infections cause positive HIV tests

Secondly, it's well understood that many endemic infections will trigger the same antibodies that cause positive reactions on the HIV antibody tests. When I asked Thuli Nxege, a 28-year-old domestic worker from a rural Zulu township, what made her neighbors sick, she cited tuberculosis, and added that the lack of sanitary facilities and having open latrine pits adjacent to village homes made it difficult to prepare clean food.

Beauty Nongila, principal of a rural school in north Zululand, insisted that having more toilets would improve the health of her 408 students (her sparsely-equipped elementary school has four). She struggled to provide her underfed kids with a spartan lunch on an allowance of 8 cents a day. When I inquired about the AIDS crisis, she laughed and said that dental problems, respiratory illnesses, diarrhea, and chronic hunger were far more vexing.

Figures about children orphaned by AIDS also bear closer examination. The average fertility rate among African women is 5.8 and the risk of death in childbirth is one in three. The African life span is not long—50 for women and 47 for men—so it would not be surprising, on a continent of 650 million people, if there were even more than 10 million children whose mothers had died before they reached high school age.

The scandal is that long-standing ailments that are largely the product of poverty are being blamed on a sexually transmitted virus. With missionary-like zeal, but without evidence, condom manufacturers and AIDS fund-raisers attribute those symptoms to an "African sexual culture." Rev. Eugene Rivers of Boston has launched a crusade to change African sexual practices—a crusade reminiscent of Victorian voyeurs whose racist constructs equated black people with sexual promiscuity.

In South Africa criticism is on the rise. Some journalists and physicians are challenging the marketing of anxieties and questioning the epidemic.

Noncontagious indigenous explanations

[In 1999] South African President Thabo Mbeki launched an investigation into the safety and benefits of AZT, a toxic and expensive drug that produces abnormalities in laboratory animals; and for which its claims of life-extending benefits remain unproved. South Africa's Minister of Health, Manto Tshabalala-Msimang (a physician herself), told South African television audiences in December that she would not recommend AZT, advice echoed on the same program by Dr. Sam Mhlongo of the National Medical University in Pretoria.

Long-standing ailments that are largely the product of poverty are being blamed on a sexually transmitted virus.

I'd argue that wearing red ribbons or issuing calls to condomize the continent will do little for the health of Africans. By contrast, a 1998 study of pregnant, HIV-positive women in Tanzania showed that simply providing them with inexpensive micronutrient supplements produced beneficial effects during and after pregnancy. The researchers found that women who received prenatal multivitamins had heavier placentas, gave birth to healthier babies, and showed a noticeable "improvement in fetal nutritional status, enhancement of fetal immunity and decreased risk of infections."

Once AIDS activists consider the non-contagious, indigenous-disease explanations for what is called AIDS, they may see things differently. The problem is that dysentery and malaria do not inspire headlines or fatten public health budgets. Infectious "plagues" do.

This means that those who question AIDS in Africa put their own funding at risk. I saw this at first-hand when I visited Swaziland . . . at the invitation of their HIV/AIDS Crisis Management Committee. I was driven from the airport to the hotel in a late model 4-wheel drive vehicle. It had been donated by UNICEF [officially, the United Nations Children's Fund] and was covered with AIDS posters urging Swazis to "use a condom, save a life." The committee included representatives of the major government ministries, as well as church and women's groups.

After my presentation, an attorney named Teresa Mlangeni acknowledged that she could easily see how malnutrition, tuberculosis, malaria, and other parasitic infections—not sexual behavior—were making her fellow Swazis ill. But other committee members confided that if they voiced public doubts, they risked losing their international funding. And I realized that the vested interests of the international AIDS orthodoxy would discourage further inquiries.

Traditional public-health approaches, clean water, and improved sanitation above all can tackle the underlying health problems in Africa. They may not be sexy, but they will save lives. And they will surely stop terrorizing an entire continent.

8

SARS Is a Continuing Threat

National Intelligence Council

The National Intelligence Council (NIC) is a federal advisory group reporting to the director of the Central Intelligence Agency (CIA). The NIC, established in 1979, produces "estimative" intelligence reports—assessments of current national security issues for senior government policy makers, and both classified and unclassified National Intelligence Estimates and Intelligence Community Assessments of the likely course and effects of social and political trends.

Severe acute respiratory syndrome, or SARS, is a highly contagious viral disease unknown in humans before late 2002. By the time the initial outbreak subsided in July 2003, SARS had infected more than eight thousand people in twenty-nine countries, killing more than 770. Medical experts believe SARS will return, as most infectious diseases do, reemerging and declining as seasonal temperatures change and as health care quarantine and treatment guidelines vary. When SARS does strike again, there is good reason to consider the disease a serious threat: There is no reliable screening test, no vaccine, no effective treatment for SARS-related pneumonia, and no well-organized control measures in poor countries whose already sick and malnourished populations are the most likely to die of the disease.

E ven though SARS [severe acute respiratory syndrome] has infected and killed far fewer people than other common infectious diseases such as influenza, malaria, tuberculosis, and HIV/AIDS, it has had a disproportionately large economic and political impact because it spread in areas with broad international commercial links and received intense media attention as a mysterious new illness that seemed able to go anywhere and hit anyone.

As the first infectious disease to emerge as a new cause of human illness in the 21st century, SARS underscores the growing importance of health issues in a globalized world. . . .

Since WHO [the World Health Organization] first issued a global alert about SARS in March 2003, almost 8,500 probable cases have been reported from 29 countries around the world, with most cases (over 7,000)

National Intelligence Council, "SARS: Down but Still a Threat," *Intelligence Community Assessment NIC ICA 2003-09*, August 2003.

occurring in China.[1] At one point in May [2003], over 180 new infections were being reported daily, mostly in China.

The number of SARS cases peaked in May and steadily declined worldwide with the WHO declaring on 5 July [2003] that all transmission chains of the disease had been broken. The decline may reflect a seasonal retreat of the disease in warmer months, which is common for respiratory illnesses in temperate climates. Nonetheless, the downturn clearly illustrates that, even in a globalized world, the old-fashioned work of identifying and isolating suspected cases, tracing and quarantining others who might be exposed, and issuing travel advisories can control an emerging disease. . . .

Basic risks of SARS

The SARS epidemic spread rapidly because people had little immunity to the newly emerged coronavirus that causes the disease. Close contact with sick individuals appears to be the primary means of virus transmission, although research indicates that SARS does not transmit as easily from person-to-person as more common diseases like the cold or flu. The disease spread most rapidly among healthcare workers and family members of infected individuals. Evidence indicates that the virus also is spread through contact with inanimate objects contaminated with virus-containing secretions. Recent detection of a related coronavirus in wildcat species in China raises concerns that SARS may continue to have an animal reservoir, which would complicate control efforts.

SARS can progress rapidly from fever and cough to serious pneumonia after an average four-to-six-day incubation period, with up to 20 percent of patients needing mechanical ventilation to survive. In some patients, progression to pneumonia may be delayed. Death may occur several weeks to months after initial symptoms.

No proven therapy is available for severe SARS pneumonia cases.

Accurate, rapid screening diagnostic tests for SARS are being developed but are not yet licensed in the United States. During the epidemic healthcare workers generally relied on clinical symptoms for detection. WHO defines a suspected SARS case as someone with a temperature over 38 degrees Celsius [100.4 degrees Fahrenheit], a cough or difficulty breathing, and one or more of the following exposures: close contact with a person who is a suspect or probable SARS case, or someone who has lived in or visited a region with SARS transmissions. A "probable case" is a suspected case with radiographic evidence of pneumonia or positive laboratory tests that may take days to weeks to complete.

No proven therapy is available for severe SARS pneumonia cases. Most clinicians employ respiratory support, antibiotics, fever reduction, and hydration. Some Chinese doctors have used steroids and the antiviral drug ribavirin with varying degrees of success.

---

1. In December 2003 WHO revised this total to 8,096.

Although the overall lethality of SARS is higher than initially believed, most deaths continue to be among older patients and those with underlying health problems, such as diabetes or hepatitis B. The WHO reported in May 2003 that death rates vary substantially by age:
- Less than 1 percent in persons 24 years or younger.
- Up to 6 percent in persons 25 to 44 years old.
- Up to 15 percent in persons 44 to 64 years old.
- Greater than 55 percent in persons aged 65 or older.

Preliminary reports on nonfatal cases showed SARS patients required longer hospital stays—an average of three weeks for those under 60 years of age—than patients with other typical respiratory viruses, raising the economic costs of the SARS outbreak. Moreover, preliminary evidence suggests that some people who survive SARS could suffer long-term respiratory damage that increases health complications and costs. . . .

Reasons to stay on guard

Despite the downturn in cases, SARS has not been eradicated and remains a significant potential threat. Senior WHO officials and many other noted medical experts believe it highly likely that SARS will return. SARS, like other respiratory diseases such as influenza, may have subsided in the northern hemisphere as summer temperatures rise, only to come back in the fall.
- Most infectious diseases follow a similar epidemiological curve, emerging, peaking, and declining over time to a steady state, but the number of infections, the lethality, and length of time can vary enormously.
- Even as WHO officials removed the last of its travel advisories for SARS [in] summer [2003], officers repeatedly emphasized the risk that the disease would be back.
- Some experts caution that SARS might even lay low for several years before reappearing, as diseases such as Ebola and Marburg have done.
- The apparent reservoir of the coronavirus in animals, Bejing's decision to lift the ban on sales of exotic animals, and lack of a reliable diagnostic kit, vaccine, or antiviral drug are factors that preclude eradication.

No reliable screening tests

Diagnosis remains almost as much an art as a science as long as no proven screening test has been developed. Diagnostic kits currently under development can catch only about 70 percent of SARS cases, and their utility for widespread deployment is not yet known. SARS is difficult to detect, particularly in the early stages, even for countries with the most modern medical capabilities, raising the risk that healthcare workers will miss mild cases. Moreover, there is little prospect of a vaccine in the short-term. . . .

SARS could mutate

Natural mutations in the coronavirus which causes SARS could alter basic characteristics of the disease, but whether a mutation would make SARS more or less dangerous is impossible to predict. A significant increase in the transmissibility or lethality of SARS obviously would pose greater health risks and raise fears around the globe.

- Mutations could be particularly problematic if they alter the symptoms associated with SARS, making it harder to identify suspected cases. . . .
- Mutations also would complicate the development of a treatment or vaccine, which already probably is several years away.

Difficult to maintain vigilance

The willingness of healthcare workers to serve in the face of significant infection risks has been a key variable in the battle against SARS and other emerging diseases. Most healthcare workers in countries hit by SARS toiled long hours under dangerous conditions. The rate of infection among hospital workers was much higher than among the general public, underscoring the difficulty even professionals had in maintaining stringent infection control procedures.

- At one point 20 percent of those infected in Hong Kong were nurses, and over 300 healthcare workers were infected within a 17-day period in China during April.

Some health workers refused to work in SARS wards. This problem is likely to grow in both rich and poor countries if the disease resurges. . . .

Despite the downturn in cases, SARS has not been eradicated and remains a significant potential threat.

Shortages in trained healthcare personnel were exacerbated when many healthcare workers fell ill to SARS and were replaced by workers with less training. . . .

Faced with these uncertainties, we have constructed three scenarios to consider potential trajectories for the disease and the implications for the United States. We have not attempted to identify a most likely scenario because the future course of SARS will depend on a host of complex variables, including the scope of present infections, mutations in the virus, the vulnerability of host populations, how individuals and governments respond, and chance.

Scenario one: SARS simmers

SARS could resurface [in 2004] but be limited to random outbreaks in a few countries. Rapid activation of local and international surveillance systems and isolation procedures would be key to identifying suspect cases and containing the spread. Initially, some cases might elude detection by hospital workers and airport personnel, who have relaxed screening procedures since the disease ebbed. Smaller, poorly-funded transit facilities would remain vulnerable because they lacked trained staff and equipment to effectively monitor all passengers.

- In most affected countries, the small number of cases and transmission would render SARS more of a public health nuisance than a crisis.

Some countries would be tempted to hide a resurgence. China's experience demonstrated that hiding an outbreak is increasingly difficult and costly in a globalized world, but some governments still probably calculate that transparency also has drawbacks. Indeed, the economic repercussions of WHO travel advisories for SARS probably reinforce the incentives countries have to hide or underreport cases.

- The WHO had to lean on Beijing throughout the crisis to share data.
- Some countries over the past decade have not acknowledged HIV/AIDS cases in the military for security reasons, suggesting they would withhold information on other diseases that might affect readiness. . . .

Paradoxically, keeping SARS out of the United States might become more difficult as fewer cases are seen, because health, transportation, and security workers are more likely to drop their guard in monitoring for infected people if only a few cases pop up now and then.

- The US status as a major hub for international travel increases the statistical risk that lapses in surveillance abroad could facilitate the spread of SARS to American cities.
- It is difficult for many visitors to acquire visas for travel to the United States; thus they probably would be inclined to withhold information that could complicate their visit.

Scenario two: SARS spreads to poor countries, regions

SARS could gain a foothold in one or more poor countries, potentially generating more infections and deaths than before but with relatively little international economic impact. Few poor countries have had SARS appear on their doorstep up to now because most have relatively few links to the affected regions, but the longer the disease persists the more likely it is that SARS will spread more widely.

- Impoverished areas of Africa, Asia, and Latin America remain at potential risk for SARS because of weak healthcare systems and vulnerable populations. Even a small number of cases in large, underdeveloped cities such as Dhaka, Kinshasa, or Lagos could generate a large number of victims in a short period.
- No evidence thus far suggests that people with malaria or HIV/AIDS are more susceptible to becoming infected by SARS, but experience indicates that diseases are more lethal among sick and malnourished populations. Sub-Saharan Africa has the highest concentration of HIV-infected people in the world, and those with full-blown AIDS have severely deficient immune response.

Most poor countries would have trouble organizing control measures against SARS, especially if the disease gained momentum before it was identified by healthcare workers. Most countries have inadequate hospital facilities to effectively isolate large numbers of patients, and most hospitals even lack the resources to provide food and care to patients.

- Voluntary home quarantine might not be viable in crowded urban slums, where large families might share small dwellings and people might have to go out each day for food or work.

- Identifying and tracking down people who might have been exposed probably would be substantially more difficult in countries with poor infrastructure and underfunded local security services.
- Repressive countries, fearful that the disease could spark political upheaval, probably would quarantine entire towns or villages with military force or incarcerate quarantine violators. Outside countries and international organizations providing assistance are likely to split over how much to condemn or withhold aid over apparent human rights violations.

The spread of SARS into various poor countries is likely to significantly disrupt local economies while having relatively little impact on broader international markets. . . .

SARS is difficult to detect . . . even for countries with the most modern medical capabilities.

The spread of SARS to poor countries also would complicate international efforts to control the disease.

- Diagnosing SARS is likely to be more difficult among populations with many preexisting health problems.
- Even if SARS claimed hundreds of victims in poor countries, their governments probably would not be inclined to devote substantial resources to the fight when other diseases—such as malaria, tuberculosis, and HIV/AIDS—were claiming many more lives.

The spread of SARS to countries with weak healthcare systems and vulnerable populations also is likely to make the disease appear more transmissible and lethal, heightening public fears in other parts of the world.

- Poor, isolated regions of Russia and China would have trouble containing an outbreak, although their governments probably could mobilize more resources to respond once infections began to climb.
- Even if SARS outbreaks were limited to poor countries, the persistence of the disease probably would fuel some unease around the world about a broader resurgence. The impact probably would marginally decrease demand for travel and increase demand for medical products.

An outbreak of SARS in poor countries would pose particular challenges for the United States and other governments and multilateral organizations providing assistance. WHO and CDC [Centers for Disease Control and Prevention] probably would come under pressure to provide money and technical assistance to compensate for weak healthcare systems. The higher the number of infected people, the more the international community would be called on to do something. . . .

Scenario three: SARS resurges in major trade centers

SARS could stage a comeback this fall in the main places it hit before—such as China, Hong Kong, Taiwan, and Canada—or gain a foothold in other places with extensive international travel and trade links like the United States, Japan, Europe, India, or Brazil. . . .

Even if the number of infected persons were not greater in a second wave, an outbreak of SARS in major trade centers again would be likely to have significant economic and political implications. The resurgence of SARS in Asia probably would cause less disruption as citizens, companies, and governments learn to live with it, as they do with other diseases, unless the transmissibility or lethality rose substantially. Nonetheless, a second wave of SARS in Asia probably would prompt some multinationals to modestly reduce their exposure to the region if they concluded that SARS posed a long-term health challenge. . . .

Bigger outbreaks in places such as Europe and the United States would affect new sets of business and government players. The level of public fear almost certainly would be higher in places that had not been affected by the first wave of SARS, driving up social disruption and economic costs.

- The economic cost of SARS probably would skyrocket if fears grow about the transmission of the disease in planes or on objects. . . .

Even the health systems of rich countries could be overwhelmed if the resurgence of SARS cases coincided with the annual influenza epidemic. . . . As long as no quick and reliable test to diagnose SARS exists people with fevers and a cough could overwhelm hospitals and clinics as healthcare workers struggled to distinguish patients with SARS and isolate them from others. . . .

The emergence of SARS has sparked widespread calls for greater international surveillance and cooperation against such diseases. SARS has demonstrated to even skeptical government leaders that health matters in profound social, economic, and political ways.

9

Antibiotic-Resistant Infectious Diseases Are a Major Threat

World Health Organization

The World Health Organization (WHO) is the United Nations special-ized agency for health, established in 1948 and based in Geneva, Switzerland. The agency monitors disease outbreaks, coordinates inter-national medical research and treatment programs, issues traveler advi-sories on vaccination and regional health risks, and advises policy mak-ers on global health trends and emergencies.

The miracle drugs of the twentieth century—penicillin, tetracycline, methicillin, vancomycin, and dozens of other antibiotics—are rapidly becoming useless against multidrug-resistant microorganisms, and ef-fective replacements do not exist. Antibiotic resistance is caused by several factors. Some resistant bacteria are created by natural muta-tion during reproduction, but other factors are due to human actions. For example, antibiotics have been overprescribed as cure-alls and are often used inappropriately. The threat of drug resistance increases when patients stop taking antibiotics too soon because not enough of the drug is ingested to kill all of the bacteria; the most resistant or-ganisms survive and reproduce. Moreover, widespread veterinary and agricultural use of antibiotics puts trace amounts of antibiotics into the food supply, which creates an environment in which resistant bacteria thrive. The result is that infectious diseases such as tuber-culosis, malaria, cholera, HIV, and gonorrhea are more lethal, and spread more rapidly, than ever before.

The History of Medicine

- 2000 B.C. Here, eat this root.
- 1000 A.D. That root is heathen. Here, say this prayer.
- 1850 A.D. That prayer is superstition. Here, drink this potion.
- 1920 A.D. That potion is snake oil. Here, swallow this pill.

World Health Organization, "Overcoming Antimicrobial Resistance," www.who.int, June 12, 2000. Copyright © 2000 by the World Health Organization. Reproduced by permission.

- 1945 A.D. That pill is ineffective. Here, take this penicillin.
- 1955 A.D. Oops . . . bugs mutated. Here, take this tetracycline.
- 1960–1999 39 more "oops". . . Here, take this more powerful antibiotic.
- 2000 A.D. The bugs have won! Here, eat this root.

—Anonymous

As early as half a century ago—just a few years after penicillin was put on the market—scientists began noticing the emergence of a penicillin-resistant strain of *Staphylococcus aureus*, a common bacterium that claims membership among the human body's normal bacterial flora. Resistant strains of gonorrhoea, dysentery-causing shigella (a major cause of premature death in developing countries) and salmonella rapidly followed in the wake of staphylococcus 20 to 25 years later.

From that first case of resistant staphylococcus, the problem of antimicrobial resistance has snowballed into a serious public health concern with economic, social and political implications that are global in scope and cross all environmental and ethnic boundaries. Multi drug-resistant tuberculosis (MDR-TB) is no longer confined to any one country or to those co-infected with HIV, but has appeared in locations as diverse as eastern Europe, Africa and Asia among health care workers and in the general population. Penicillin-resistant pneumococci are likewise spreading rapidly, while resistant malaria is on the rise, disabling and killing millions of children and adults each year. In 1990, almost all cholera isolates gathered around New Delhi (India) were sensitive to cheap, first-line drugs furazolidone, ampicillin, co-trimoxazole and nalidixic acid. Now, 14 years later, formerly effective drugs are largely useless in the battle to contain cholera epidemics.

In some areas of the world—most notably South-East Asia—98% of all gonorrhoea cases are multi drug-resistant, which in turn contributes to the sexual transmission of HIV. In India, 60% of all cases of visceral leishmaniasis—a sandfly-borne parasitic infection—no longer respond to an increasingly limited cache of first-line drugs; while in the industrialized world, as many as 60% of hospital-acquired infections are caused by drug-resistant microbes. These infections—the most recent of which are vancomycin-resistant *Enterococcus* (VRE) and methicillin-resistant *Staphylococcus aureus* (MRSA), are now no longer confined to wards but have crept into the community at large.

Although most drugs are still active, the lengthening shadow of resistance means that many of them may not be for long. In the case of tuberculosis, the emergence of multi drug-resistant bacteria means that medications that once cost as little as US$ 20 must now be replaced with drugs a hundred times more expensive. Other diseases are likewise becoming increasingly impervious as currently effective drugs continue to be underused by patients who do not complete courses, and misused through indiscriminate and over-prescribing. . . .

How resistance develops and spreads

Researchers [know] that pathogens develop resistance to antimicrobials through a process known as natural selection. When a microbial population is exposed to an antibiotic, more susceptible organisms will succumb, leaving behind only those resistant to the antimicrobial onslaught. These organisms can then either pass on their resistance genes to their offspring by replication, or to other related bacteria through "conjugation" whereby plasmids carrying the genes "jump" from one organism to another. This process is a natural, unstoppable phenomenon exacerbated by the abuse, overuse and misuse of antimicrobials in the treatment of human illness and in animal husbandry, aquaculture and agriculture. Disease—and therefore resistance—also thrives in conditions of civil unrest, poverty, mass migration and environmental degradation where large numbers of people are exposed to infectious diseases with little in the way of the most basic health care. . . .

The problem of antimicrobial resistance has snowballed into a serious public health concern.

More than any other issue, poverty and inadequate access to drugs continue to be a major force in the development of resistance. In many developing nations drugs are freely available—but only to those who can afford them. This means that most patients are forced to resort to poor quality, counterfeit, or truncated treatment courses that invariably lead to more rapid selection of resistant organisms. A patient infected with a resistant strain may endure prolonged illness (often resulting in death) and hospital stays which in turn result in lost wages, lost productivity, family hardship and increased infectiousness. Treatment with second and third-line drugs is costly, more often toxic to the patient, and increasingly ineffective owing to the speed with which mutant organisms develop resistance. In India, the past five years has seen 20% of typhoid isolates become resistant to ciprofloxacin, a relatively recent and expensive third-line drug.

Misdiagnosis and resistance

Misdiagnosis is just another symptom of weak public health systems in industrialized and developing nations. Overworked and under-informed physicians and healthcare workers are ill-equipped to deal with the large number of patients pouring through clinic and office doors. Increased pressure inevitably leads to "defensive" and unnecessary prescribing as a means of forestalling potential complications. A dearth of proper diagnostic facilities and laboratories in poorer nations means physicians and healthcare workers are forced to engage in the kind of symptom-based guesswork that often leads to misdiagnosis and the increased likelihood of prescribing the wrong medication. In many developing countries poverty and a lack of information forces patients to purchase single doses of drugs taken only until the patient feels better. Health workers may also be responsible. In a study undertaken in Viet Nam in 1997, researchers discovered that more than 70% of patients were prescribed inadequate amounts of antimicrobials for serious infections, while another 25% were given unnecessary antibiotics. In China, researchers found that 63% of antimicrobials selected to treat proven bacterial infections were simply the wrong choice, while in Bangladesh 50% of drugs dispensed in one hospital unit were inappropriate. The same is true in North America where it is estimated that physicians in both Canada and the United States over-prescribe antibiotics by 50%. . . .

Resistance flourishes wherever antibiotics are abused, misused and dispensed at levels lower than treatment guidelines dictate. This means that instead of wiping out the infection altogether, medications kill only non-resistant organisms—leaving their tougher counterparts to replicate and spread resistant genes. . . .

Antimicrobial resistance and food

Another source of resistance lies in our food supply and is related to infectious agents that live in what we eat and drink. Since the discovery of the growth-promoting and disease-fighting capabilities of antibiotics, farmers, fish-farmers and livestock producers have used antimicrobials in everything from apples to aquaculture. Currently, only half of all antibiotics produced are slated for human consumption. The other 50% are used to treat sick animals, as growth promoters in livestock, and to rid cultivated foodstuffs of various destructive organisms. This ongoing and often low-level dosing for growth and prophylaxis inevitably results in the development of resistance in bacteria in or near livestock, and also heightens fears of new resistant strains "jumping" between species. Vancomycin-resistant *Enterococcus faecium* (VRE) is one particularly ominous example of a resistant bacterium appearing in animals that may have "jumped" into more vulnerable segments of the human population.

The emergence of VRE in food can be traced to the widespread use of avoparcin (the animal equivalent of the human antibiotic vancomycin) in livestock. Moreover, with livestock production increasing in developing countries, reliance on antimicrobials is likewise expanding—often without guidelines in those nations where antibiotics are sold without prescription. With the trends toward globalization and the relaxing of trade barriers, inadequate standards and enforcement in one nation means all others are vulnerable.

Formerly effective drugs are largely useless in the battle to contain cholera epidemics.

Often bacteria that are harmless to livestock are fatal to humans. This is true of a number of outbreaks that have taken the medical community by surprise. One example occurred in Denmark in 1998, when strains of multi drug-resistant *Salmonella typhimurium* struck 25 people, killing two. Cultures confirmed that the organisms were resistant to seven different antibiotics. Epidemiologists eventually traced the micro-organism to pork and to the pig herd where it originated. In 1998, 5,000 people in the United States learned the hard way about antimicrobial resistance when they fell ill with multi drug-resistant campylobacteriosis caused by contaminated chicken. The same drugs that eventually failed them had also been used in the poultry that turned up on their plates. . . .

As quickly as new drugs are launched to smash humanity's most intractable infectious enemies, the forces of resistance regroup and strike back with yet another counter-offensive.

Pneumonia

More than any other infectious disease, pneumonia remains the number one killer worldwide. Statistics for 1998 show that 3.5 million people died as a result of the disease. The majority of all acute respiratory infections (ARIs) occur in developing countries where poverty and inadequate medical care contribute to high mortality rates. The primary microbial culprits, *Streptococcus pneumoniae* and *Haemophilus influenzae*, have, thus far, proven themselves wily opponents. In lab samples as many as 70% of chest infections are resistant to one of the first-line antimicrobials. These numbers will only increase the longer action is delayed. Formerly, first-line medications were both effective and affordable. With the onset of resistance however, newer treatments are proving too costly to the vast majority of those living in poor developing nations. This alarming situation is due, in part, to widespread confusion over the difference between viral and bacterial respiratory infections. Both forms present the same clinical symptoms that can often only be distinguished by laboratory tests—expensive and therefore unavailable in many parts of the world. While bacterial infections can kill, treating viral illness with antibiotics is not only ineffective but contributes to the development of resistance. This is particularly true when it comes to treating children. Recent studies undertaken by WHO indicate that for every 100 respiratory infections, only 20% require antibiotic treatment. This means that 80% of patients are treated with unnecessary medications thereby leading drugs directly into the sight lines of resistance. . . .

Diarrhoeal diseases

Multi drug-resistance is also occurring in microbes that cause diarrhoeal diseases. Combined, these infections are believed to have claimed the lives of more than 2.2 million people in 1998. One such agent, the bacterium *Shigella dysenteriae*, is a highly virulent microbe that is resistant to almost every available drug—killing adults and children alike. The results of this growing crisis were illustrated most notably in the wake of the 1994 civil war in Rwanda when the bacterium spread through vulnerable refugee populations already traumatized by war and loss. Left untreated, death can follow within days of infection. Ten years ago a shigella epidemic could easily be controlled with co-trimoxazole—a drug cheaply available in generic form. Today, nearly all shigella are non-responsive to the drug, while resistance to ciprofloxacin—the only viable medication left—appears to be just around the corner. Shigella dysentery is rare in developed countries, and thus, not a pressing concern to pharmaceutical companies favouring higher returns on research and development.

The bacteria that cause cholera and typhoid are also revealing the ease with which they acquire resistance. In treating people with cholera, fluid replacement is paramount, but antibiotics (especially tetracycline) play an important public health role in limiting the spread of epidemics. Salmonella typhi—like shigella,—is adept at accumulating cassettes of resistance genes, producing strains that withstand fast-line, second-line and now, third-line drugs. Up until 1972, chloramphenicol was the treatment of choice for typhoid fever throughout much of the Indian subcontinent. By 1992 two-thirds of reported cases were chloramphenicol-resistant, thereby necessitating treatment with expensive quinolones that are themselves losing effectiveness. Without proper treatment, typhoid is a serious and frequently relapsing disease that kills up to 10% of those infected.

AIDS

At the end of 1999, an estimated 33.6 million individuals were living with HIV worldwide. In Zimbabwe, up to 50% of pregnant women are infected with HIV, while in Botswana life expectancy has plummeted from 70 to 50 years in the past 25 years because of AIDS. Worldwide, some 2.6 million people died in 1999 as a result of infection with HIV.

Although most drugs are still active, the lengthening shadow of resistance means that many of them may not be for long.

Because of inadequate access, infected individuals are often unable to obtain antiretroviral drugs. This bleak scenario will continue as a growing number of HIV-infected individuals develop AIDS. For these people—particularly the bulk of those living in developing nations—the availability of HIV tests and expensive life-prolonging drug cocktails are largely nonexistent—until now. Moreover, in the industrialized world—where treatment is more readily available—drug combinations are under increasing pressure to remain viable owing to both resistance and toxic side-effects. A small but growing number of patients are showing primary resistance to zidovudine (AZT)—as opposed to "secondary" resistance where viruses grow increasingly insensitive to antivirals over the course of the patient's illness. This is also true for protease inhibitors that became available a mere 10 years ago. A growing body of evidence indicates that when HIV develops resistance to one protease inhibitor it quickly becomes insensitive to the entire family of drugs, thus outwitting antiretrovirals that took years to develop at huge cost. AIDS is a particularly insidious disease because those infected become reservoirs for TB, leishmaniasis, pneumonia and other opportunistic infections—some of which have themselves developed resistance. These infections are transmissible to the population at large.

Tuberculosis

Tuberculosis is yet another ancient killer that is not only staging a major comeback, but is becoming increasingly resistant to anti-TB drugs. Exact figures for MDR-TB are hard to pin down as surveillance remains uneven in nations most affected. Nevertheless, researchers assess the approximate number of multi drug-resistant TB cases at between 1% and 2% of current global tuberculosis figures. This apparently low figure may suggest that there is less cause for alarm unless the overall prevalence of TB—estimated to be 16 million cases—is recognized. Fears will continue as nations where MDR-TB went previously unreported—China, The Islamic Republic of Iran and parts of eastern Europe—reveal a growing caseload. Recent reports of global trends in MDR-TB are particularly chilling when one considers that tuberculosis is transmitted by tiny particles suspended in the air.

Adding to the resistance crisis is the length of TB treatments (a minimum of six months), with non-compliance common in those living in nations unable or unwilling to adopt the WHO-recommended Directly Observed Treatment, Short-course (DOTS). Consistently applied, DOTS can cure disease in upwards of 95% of drug-susceptible cases—even in impoverished nations. This strategy not only ensures a cure by directly supervising and adapting drugs to patient needs, but also minimizes the development of resistance by preventing treatment failure. Treatment failures occur when patients are either dosed with poor quality drugs, have limited access to, or are non-compliant with existing therapies. Insufficient treatment results in a roller-coaster ride of brief reprieves followed by relapses that grow ever more impregnable to available medications each time the TB organism rallies. Currently, a single treatment course of six months for regular tuberculosis costs as little as US$ 20. With MDR-TB, the costs shoot upward to US$ 2,000, or even more.

In the post-Perestroika era of eastern Europe and the Russian Federation, inadequate treatment—i.e. poor monitoring, interrupted courses, or a reliance on expired or counterfeit drugs—corresponds to growing transmission rates of resistant TB organisms.

Tuberculosis is yet another ancient killer that is not only staging a major comeback, but is becoming increasingly resistant to anti-TB drugs.

In addition, patients who are infected with HIV, have silicosis, are diabetic, or are immune-compromised in any way, are more vulnerable to TB exposure and become unwitting pools of infectiousness that easily spills over into the general population.

The ability of HIV to accelerate the onset of acute MDR-TB has serious implications for humanity. In crowded hospitals filled with immunosuppressed individuals, resistant TB has the potential to stalk relentlessly through a population, afflicting patients, health care workers and physicians alike. War, poverty, overcrowding, mass migration and the breakdown of existing medical infrastructures all contribute to MDR-TB's development, transmission and spread.

Malaria

A mosquito-borne infection that killed an estimated 1.1 million people in 1998, and with an estimated 300 to 400 million new cases globally each year, malaria promises to be a pre-eminent threat to development in endemic regions well into the new millennium.

Like other diseases once considered banished to the geopolitical margins, malaria is reappearing in areas of the world formerly deemed disease-free. In a 1999 report WHO warned of "a serious risk of uncontrollable resurgence of malaria" in Europe owing to civil disorder, global warming, increased irrigation (canals are important breeding grounds for mosquitoes) and international travel. In the United Kingdom, 1,000 new cases of malaria are imported each year from malaria-endemic countries. In the former USSR, weakening public infrastructures have triggered large-scale epidemics in central Asian republics, while in Turkey numbers have increased tenfold since the disease was believed nearly defeated in 1989.

Resistance to chloroquine—the former treatment of choice—is now widespread in 80% of the 92 countries where malaria continues to be a major killer, while resistance to newer second and third-line drugs continues to grow. Unfortunately, many of these new drugs are not only expensive and have serious side effects, but most will be eventually rendered ineffective by the malaria organism's complex epidemiology and facility for rapid mutation. Mefloquine resistance emerged in SouthEast Asia almost as soon as the drug became a treatment option.

Resistance to chloroquine—the former treatment of choice—is now widespread in 80% of the 92 countries where malaria continues to be a major killer.

The challenge is to use already existing antimalarials more effectively to better control the disease. This means improving access to appropriate drugs and providing combinations of medications at lower cost. Increasing surveillance to guide the proper use of drugs, and more attention to alternative prevention strategies such as insecticide-treated bednets is also vital. A renewed commitment to research and development of newer, more effective medications is likewise critical to the containment of drug-resistant malaria. . . .

Hospital-acquired infections

No population is more vulnerable to multi drug-resistance than those admitted to hospital wards. Of the resistant organisms now proliferating around the world, none carry more potential for destruction and threaten existing medical interventions than the emergence of hospital-acquired "super-infections". In the United States alone, some 14,000 individuals are infected and die each year from drug-resistant microbes picked up in hospital. Salmonella, Pseudomonas and Klebsiella are among the bacteria manifesting high levels of resistance—most notably in developing nations. Other infections—for instance methicillin-resistant *Staphyloccocus aureus* (MRSA) and vancomycin-resistant *Enterococcus* (VRE)—are also wreaking havoc in hospital wards around the world. During the 1950s and 1960s most staphylococcus infections were penicillin-sensitive. Now, at the beginning of the new millennium, almost all are not only resistant to penicillin, but also increasingly impervious to each successive drug developed to breach the gap.

From what used to be considered mere medical curiosities, these resistant infections have exploded into a major healthcare crisis. In some hospitals—particularly in the United States—most staphylococcus and enterococcus infections are increasingly intractable. So far, the only drug available to treat MRSA is vancomycin—itself faltering in the face of a renewed attack by vancomycin-intermediate *Staphyloccocus aureus*, otherwise known as VISA. This emerging microbe is already showing levels of resistance that, while still manageable, are nonetheless threatening to catapult it into the drug-resistant big leagues.

Of the resistant organisms now proliferating around the world, none carry more potential for destruction . . . than . . . hospital-acquired "super-infections".

Because hospitals and nursing homes typically hold large numbers of immuno-compromised patients—specifically those individuals who have recently undergone transplants, are taking cancer treatment or have been infected with HIV—organisms usually considered harmless in healthy individuals proliferate uncontested by the body's immune response. So far, current preventive methods emphasizing hygiene and aggressive infection-control measures have reaped only dubious benefits and at best, only slowed the spread of resistant bacteria. This means that commonplace medical procedures once previously taken for granted—hip replacements, dental surgery and cyst removals—could conceivably be consigned to medical limbo. The repercussions are almost unimaginable.

An added concern is that hospital-acquired infections rarely stay put. Ample evidence would suggest that many resistant infections erupted in hospital settings before migrating to the community at large. Already, both MRSA and VRE have spread outside the hospital to affect healthy populations. . . .

Gonorrhoea

Gonorrhoea is one example of how antimicrobial abuse has propelled a once-curable nuisance into a potentially life-threatening contagion. The development of antimicrobial resistance in gonorrhoea is one of the major health care disasters of the 20th century.

Gonorrhoea and other sexually transmitted infections (STIs) are important co-factors in the transmission and spread of HIV. This is because HIV bonds to white blood cells collecting at inflamed sites around the urino-genital tract. Studies show that those co-infected with gonorrhoea and HIV shed HIV at nine times the rate of individuals affected with HIV alone.

Of the STIs—including chancroid and chlamydial infection—gonorrhoea is the most resilient with a resistance rate that continues to outstrip new treatment strategies. Gonorrhoea resistance first showed up in GIs during the Viet Nam war and is now entrenched around the globe with MDR strains appearing in 60% of those infected each year. In most of South-East Asia, resistance to penicillin has been reported in nearly all strains at a rate of 98% overall. Newer, more expensive drugs—notably ciprofloxacin—are likewise showing an increasing failure rate. Owing to resistance gonorrhoea has become a driving force in the HIV epidemic.

Economics play a significant role in the development of gonorrhoeal resistance. For example, a 125 mg dose of ciprofloxacin may cure gonorrhoea, but will likely kill only those organisms susceptible to the medication, leaving a small number of resistant organisms that cause no symptoms. The recommended dose is 250 mg, while 500 mg will most certainly eradicate any lingering infection. The reality, however, is that poverty forces both health care providers and their patients to opt for lower doses of prescribed medications or choose cheaper, less effective alternatives in order to save money.

10

Sexually Transmitted Diseases Are a Serious Social and Economic Threat

David J. Landry and Wendy Turnbull

David J. Landry is a senior research associate with the Alan Guttmacher Institute, a nonprofit organization devoted to sexual and reproductive health research, education, and policy analysis. Wendy Turnbull is a public policy associate with the institute.

Sexually transmitted diseases (STDs) are at epidemic levels around the world, infecting more than 400 million people every year. The more than twenty diseases classified as STDs are a serious problem not only because they are so widespread but because most have long-lasting harmful health consequences, several are incurable, and at least one—AIDS—is deadly. Groups at highest risk of contracting an STD are infants born to STD-infected mothers, people with multiple sexual partners, and teenagers.

Improving the health conditions of individuals and families in the developing world has long been a priority for American humanitarian aid. As a result of 30 years of U.S. assistance, maternal and infant death rates have dropped in many regions, significantly more couples are using contraceptives to plan their families and more children are living past their fifth birthday.

Nevertheless, despite the tremendous progress brought about by investments in maternity care, family planning, child immunization and better nutrition, one crucial element of maternal and child health has been sorely neglected: the prevention and treatment of sexually transmitted diseases (STDs). Historically, STDs have also been overlooked in the global fight against infectious diseases; as a result, they continue to drain the lives of young and old throughout the developing world.

The vast majority of STDs are spread through sexual intercourse—which is perhaps the most important reason for the lack of public discourse on their impact—and women of childbearing age (15–44) are disproportionately affected. In addition, each year, millions of infants begin their lives disadvantaged by an STD they contracted from their mother; STD infections in newborns compromise their health, both immediately and in the coming years.

Long-term consequences

STDs are a serious problem not only because they are widespread, but also because they may have delayed, long-term consequences, including poor maternal health, ectopic pregnancy, infant illness and death, cervical cancer, infertility and increased susceptibility to HIV. Millions of men and women suffering these and other effects of STDs are hindered in their ability to provide for their families and contribute to their society. For countries struggling to develop economically, the health and economic costs are immense.

The toll of STDs also hampers U.S. international aid. American assistance aimed at improving educational, health and economic conditions overseas becomes less effective, and therefore more costly, when a substantial proportion of recipients are suffering from STDs. Thus, although this is not always well understood by policymakers and the public, the United States has a considerable stake in combating the burgeoning STD epidemic in developing countries. . . .

STDs are widespread

Worldwide, more than 400 million adults become infected with an STD every year. Four STDs that are spread primarily through heterosexual contact are completely curable—trichomoniasis, chlamydia, syphilis and gonorrhea. These account for 333 million STD infections, or about 80% of the worldwide total. Some 9% of all persons aged 15–44 in North America contract one of these STDs annually, but the rate rises to 25% in Sub-Saharan Africa. Trichomoniasis alone has been detected in more than 40% of women attending prenatal clinics in Uganda and Botswana.

> *Historically, STDs have . . . been overlooked in the global fight against infectious diseases; as a result, they continue to drain the lives of young and old.*

Every day, about 16,000 people (or nearly six million people each year) become infected with HIV, a startling number, given the short period of time since the virus emerged. Some nations have been hit harder than others. Among developing nations, for example, the United Nations estimates that more than 20 million people in Sub-Saharan Africa are HIV-positive, and most are unaware of their infection. While fewer than 1% of India's adults have the virus, India has the largest number of HIV-infected people in the world: 3–5 million, 89% of whom are younger than 45.

Globally, women and children represent a large proportion of those infected with HIV: In 1997, an estimated 36% of new HIV infections occurred among women; 10% were among children younger than 15. In

Latin America, HIV infections among women and teenagers, who contract the disease primarily through heterosexual intercourse, have been increasing sharply. Throughout Africa, heterosexual intercourse was responsible for an estimated 85% of new HIV infections in 1997.

Striking young adults

Because STDs strike relatively young persons and treatment often is not sought or is inaccessible, delayed or inadequate, the impact of these infections on individuals' health is high. The impact on society also is substantial, since STDs affect primarily men and women who are forming families and contributing to the work force. The World Bank and the World Health Organization have led efforts to develop measures to quantify the burden of disease. One of the best-known measures is the number of healthy years of life lost as a result of illness or premature death.

Each year, STDs, including HIV, account for 6% of healthy years of life lost among women aged 15–44 worldwide. The annual occurrence of four STDs—syphilis, gonorrhea, chlamydia and HIV—along with pelvic inflammatory disease (PID), a result of some STDs that often leads to sterility among women, accounts for the loss of more than 51 million years of healthy life among men, women and children worldwide. Women lose a disproportionate share of healthy years of life to STDs, largely because of PID.

Symbiotic STDs

A mutually reinforcing link exists between HIV and other, more common STDs. One of the principal reasons HIV prevalence is so high in developing countries is that STD levels were high before the epidemic. The susceptibility of people to HIV infection is 2–9 times as high if they already have certain infections, particularly syphilis and chancroid. Similarly, HIV facilitates the transmission, hampers the diagnosis and accelerates the progression of other STDs. For example, human papilloma virus—which is closely associated with cervical cancer—progresses at a much faster rate in HIV-infected women than in others.

Early and effective treatment of STDs, especially those that result in genital ulcers, can reduce the incidence of HIV infection. In one Tanzanian community, a program that allowed for the diagnosis and treatment of STDs without using expensive laboratory tests reduced HIV incidence by about 40%.

Groups at greatest risk

Women. A variety of biological and social factors make women more susceptible to STDs than men. Women are physiologically more vulnerable than are men to contracting STDs when they have unprotected sex (i.e., without using a condom) with an infected partner. Additionally, STDs in women are more likely to be asymptomatic; if women are unaware of their infection, they will not seek timely care and hence may experience serious complications. Further, the use of traditional vaginal medications and douching may increase a woman's risk of acquiring an STD. With the exception of HIV, STDs may have more life-threatening consequences for women (PID, ectopic pregnancy and cervical cancer, for example) than for men.

Married and monogamous women are often at higher risk of contracting STDs than might be expected, because of the high-risk behaviors that are relatively common among men in many countries: intercourse with multiple partners and with commercial sex workers. Moreover, in some countries, women's low social and educational status conspire to deny the majority of them the power and knowledge to protect themselves against STDs. In many cultures, few women are able to negotiate the conditions of their sexual lives or the effective use of protective measures with a partner. In fact, many women consider STD-related symptoms such as abdominal pain or vaginal discharge a normal condition, not realizing that their suffering is caused by a contagious disease and can be treated.

Infants of Infected Mothers. Infants born to women with an active STD are highly likely to be infected before, during or after delivery. Globally, the probability that the mother's HIV infection will be transmitted to the infant at birth ranges from about 20% to 40%; this mode of transmission accounts for 5–10% of all HIV infections worldwide. The consequences of STD infection are serious for the newborn: stillbirth or prematurity, permanent damage to vital organs and possibly death.

Should an infant manage to escape STD infection at birth, he or she is likely to feel the impact of the disease in other ways. By the end of 1997, more than eight million children had lost their mother or both parents as a result of AIDS before they had reached the age of 15. Further, untreated STDs can severely impair parents' ability to work outside the home and provide for their family adequately, increasing the risks to their children's health and well-being.

Worldwide, more than 400 million adults become infected with an STD every year.

Teenagers. Sexually active teenagers, especially males, tend to engage in riskier behavior than adults: They have more partners, have more high-risk partners and often do not use condoms. Consequently, sexually active teenagers, along with adults younger than 25, generally have the highest STD rates of any age-group. Married adolescent women who themselves may be monogamous are at risk of acquiring STDs if their husbands have sexual encounters outside the marriage.

Additionally, biological and social factors heighten the risk for young girls and teenage women. Young women contract STDs more easily than adults because they have fewer protective antibodies and the immaturity of their cervix facilitates the transmission of an infection. In some societies, sexual coercion has emerged as a major risk factor for young girls; many are forced to have sex or are given gifts or money in exchange for sex, precisely because they are seen as being disease-free.

Youth who are infected with an incurable STD—genital warts, herpes or HIV—bear the debilitating effects of the disease for the rest of their lives. Many become infertile and are unable to have families of their own.

What is needed?

STD prevention efforts are critical and should be of highest priority for policymakers, a 1997 Word Bank report declared. The sooner developing countries act to contain the spread of STDs, especially HIV, the more manageable and less severe the problem will be in future years. In particular, the Bank concluded, reaching groups most prone to spread STDs (such as sex workers, their customers and youth) with prevention programs will have the largest impact in reducing infection rates throughout a population.

In a number of countries, national prevention campaigns, using a variety of messages targeted for specific audiences, have proven effective in helping people adopt healthier behaviors. Messages that should be promoted widely among the general public include the importance of reducing the number of sexual partners, the effectiveness of condoms in protecting against infection and the benefit of dual method use, or simultaneously using a condom to prevent STD transmission and another contraceptive method to prevent unintended pregnancy.

A variety of biological and social factors make women more susceptible to STDs than men.

How and in what clinical settings STD-related counseling and medical services might best be offered are less clear. These questions have long bedeviled health advocates and policymakers. In the United States, for a variety of reasons, largely separate networks of family planning clinics and STD clinics have evolved. Recently, this two-track system has come under criticism; opponents urge that whenever possible, STD prevention, screening and treatment services be fully integrated within family planning and primary care settings, which are considered conducive to providing counseling and services to help individuals meet their pregnancy and STD prevention needs.

In developing countries, where the existing formal health system may provide inadequate or no STD services, there is an opportunity to think through these infrastructure issues from the beginning, with an eye toward developing a more integrated, comprehensive approach to STD care.

The global response

The extent of STDs and their impact on families and society first received formal recognition from the world community at the 1994 United Nations–sponsored International Conference on Population and Development, held in Cairo. At this historic gathering, policymakers pledged to focus on individuals' reproductive and sexual health needs. Such a focus, they agreed, would enable women, men and young people to lead healthier and more productive lives, and would, in turn, promote sustainable development and lower population growth rates.

The key question facing policymakers is how—and, to some extent, whether—they can fulfill their financial commitments to ensure that individuals most in need will have access to a full range of reproductive health care services. In addition to family planning, these include STD screening and treatment, maternity and postpartum care, safe abortion (where the procedure is legal) and routine gynecologic care. At the Cairo conference, both donor and developing country governments pledged new funds to fight STDs, yet that promise has gone largely unrealized, in part because U.S. political and financial leadership in the reproductive health field has faltered in recent years.

The U.S. challenge

Beginning in 1995, the long-simmering legislative feud over domestic abortion policies spilled over to the international arena, wreaking havoc with U.S. family planning and reproductive health care efforts overseas. [Since 1995] Congress has imposed deep funding cuts on the U.S. Agency for International Development's population assistance program, effectively scuttling its expansion into the provision of more comprehensive STD services. Continued funding at these depressed levels means that, in developing countries, far fewer resources will be available for STD care in family planning settings and that the burden of STDs will continue to fall on the primary caregivers and household managers—women.

Clearly, there is a compelling need for STD services. For decades, U.S. lawmakers have acknowledged the fundamental role of disease prevention and treatment in social and economic development, which remains a cornerstone of American foreign assistance. To the detriment of millions, however, the long-term impact of STDs has gone unnoticed.

Fortunately, times are changing. The global consensus that emerged in Cairo recognizes the toll of STDs on individuals and society overall, but the funding to carry out this new public health mandate is crucial. The United States was instrumental in shaping this enlightened worldview and should endeavor to follow through on its political and financial commitments to STD prevention and treatment. The quality of life for individuals and families worldwide will be greatly enhanced.

11

The Smallpox Threat Warrants Mass Vaccination

William J. Bicknell and Kenneth D. Bloem

William J. Bicknell is professor of international health at Boston University's School of Public Health and chairman emeritus of the Department of International Health. He served as Massachusetts commissioner of public health from 1972 to 1975. Kenneth D. Bloem, former CEO of Stanford University Hospital and Georgetown University Medical Center, participated in the smallpox eradication program in the Congo and Bangladesh.

Mass vaccination of healthy adults to combat smallpox is safe. In the event of a deliberate bioterrorist smallpox attack, U.S. public health agencies are simply not prepared to identify and vaccinate exposed individuals and their contacts effectively, which will lead to the spread of the disease and many unnecessary deaths. Pre-event vaccination of health care workers and the general public, in contrast, could be conducted in a systematic and orderly way, protecting a vulnerable American population with an extremely low risk of side effects.

The September 11, 2001, terrorist attacks, followed by several anthrax mailings in the fall of 2001, forced many Americans to recognize their vulnerability to various bioterrorist threats. Smallpox, in particular, had a long history as a devastating disease before its eradication in the 1970s. Recently, it has captured the attention of homeland security planners, who view it as one of the most likely and deadliest agents for bioterrorism. Federal government officials initially considered a program of modest pre-exposure vaccination to protect against deliberate release of the smallpox virus by bioterrorists. That approach was superceded when the White House announced a more ambitious plan on December 13, 2002.

Phase I of [George W. Bush's] plan called for the voluntary vaccination of approximately 500,000 health workers, 18 years old and older, by mid-January 2003.

Phase II called for the voluntary vaccination of up to 10,000,000

William J. Bicknell and Kenneth D. Bloem, "Smallpox and Bioterrorism: Why the Plan to Protect the Nation Is Stalled and What to Do," *Cato Institute Briefing Paper*, vol. 85, September 5, 2003.

health and emergency workers in the following 90 days.

Phase III, to begin in mid-2003, would make the vaccine available to, but not recommended for, the general adult population.

The plan also called for the immediate vaccination of up to 500,000 members of the armed forces. As of June 25, 2003, the military had vaccinated more than 450,000 individuals; the civilian program had vaccinated only 37,971 people by July 18. Some states had suspended their programs while awaiting guidance from the Centers for Disease Control and Prevention (CDC) on how to screen for cardiac conditions. In the District of Columbia, 105 people have been vaccinated, in Chicago 70, and in Massachusetts 120. The civilian numbers are not reassuring. . . .

A healthy adult is 42,000 times more likely to die from an accident in the next 10 years than from a smallpox vaccination.

When Phases I and II are completed, whether the event is small and inept or major and multi-focal, the nation will be well prepared to rapidly respond to and stop an outbreak of smallpox. If and as the general adult public opts for voluntary vaccination in Phase III, post-exposure control becomes even easier and faster. There will be fewer people to vaccinate, and, as the number of people susceptible to smallpox will be reduced, disease transmission will be slowed.

Does the president's plan make sense?

The answer is yes. Why is the plan sensible? First, it is phased and selective. Limiting vaccination to healthy adults dramatically reduces the risk of serious vaccine side effects. Second, by starting with 500,000 military personnel and a similar number of civilians, we develop current data about the risks of vaccination and can easily modify the plan if actual risks exceed those expected. Third, when Phase II is complete, there will be enough people vaccinated to vaccinate the balance of the population on a voluntary basis within 10 days from the time the first case is identified. Finally, and of great importance, hospitals and emergency services will be able to continue to operate while intensive mass vaccination is taking place. After an outbreak is recognized, the vast majority of people are highly likely to accept voluntary vaccination. At that point there will probably be no need for mandatory vaccination and its attendant problems.

The pre-attack plan is correctly limited to healthy adults, as the risk of serious complications and death from vaccination is substantially higher in children. However, the age for vaccination could safely be dropped to 10 years, as the overwhelming majority of deaths and severe complications from vaccination occur in children 9 years of age or younger. If we are prepared to vaccinate rapidly after an attack, children can be isolated at home for a few days until they can be vaccinated. This approach avoids a number of serious and some fatal complications of vaccination in children that would likely occur if done pre-attack, while minimizing smallpox cases and deaths post-attack. . . .

Bioterrorism, particularly with smallpox, became a pressing U.S. and international issue after September 11, 2001. The call for pre-exposure vaccination came quickly. The head of Russia's Vektor Institute, which has functions similar to those of the CDC, urged widespread immunization against smallpox. The British government bought enough vaccine for 50 percent of the population. Germany purchased 6 million doses, and Israel vaccinated approximately 18,000 first responders and medical workers. The U.S. government considered the threat sufficient to purchase vaccine and vaccinia immune globulin (VIG) for all Americans in preparation for a possible smallpox attack. By late 2002 the United States had sufficient smallpox vaccine to immunize and VIG to manage the complications of vaccination for the entire population. . . .

A careful review of historical and current data supports the conclusion that when healthy adults are vaccinated, persistent, serious side effects are extremely rare. . . .

The death rate in healthy adults may be as low as 1 in 15,000,000 vaccinees. It is quite possible, and would not be surprising, that when Phase II of the national plan is completed, we will have no deaths of persons voluntarily vaccinated, and it is likely we will have fewer than five deaths. The current U.S. military experience with 454,856 vaccinated personnel as of June 11, 2003, (71 percent were primary vaccinees and 29 percent were revaccinees) with no deaths and no long-lasting complications strongly supports the conclusion that vaccination of healthy adults is safe. . . .

Assuming Phase II of the national plan is fully completed and 10 million healthy adults are vaccinated, we estimate the number of people who may die because of accidental vaccination by exposure to a recently vaccinated person at less than one. Stated somewhat differently, most likely, no one will die. As there are an increased number of immunocompromised persons at risk of death from accidental transmission today, it is necessary to correct and increase this estimate. However, the estimate must be increased by *more than a* factor of 20 to reach one death. . . .

The bottom line: Voluntarily vaccinating healthy, well-screened adults, using the semi-permeable membrane dressing for all who get vaccinated—not just health care workers—and urging all vaccinees to wear long sleeves until their vaccination scab falls off makes the national plan safe for everyone. . . .

Comparing everyday risks and vaccine risks

We would not expect adults to get revaccinated more frequently than once in 10 years since the protection lasts about that long. Over the same 10-year time period, the risk of death from an accident of any type for an adult in America is 3/1000 or 3,000/1,000,000. Thus, a healthy adult is 42,000 times more likely to die from an accident in the next 10 years than from a smallpox vaccination! The risk of death on a scheduled domestic major airline is between 1 in 8 million and 1 in 10 million. A healthy adult has less risk of death from a smallpox vaccination than from flying from Denver to Washington, D.C. And, as flying is far safer than driving, when most of us drive to work, to the movies, or to a vacation destination voluntarily, we expose ourselves and our companions to far more risk than a smallpox vaccination does.

The bottom line: vaccination of healthy adults is safe. In our judgment, the best policy guidance that the CDC can offer is: if you are a healthy adult who does not worry about driving to work, you should not worry about getting vaccinated or accidentally vaccinating another person. . . .

Correcting misperceptions of vaccine risk

Medical and public health practitioners and the general public have received inadequate and confusing information about the risk of smallpox vaccination to healthy adults. Because healthy adults are the only group targeted in the national plan, this is a serious omission. CDC has never adequately distinguished between healthy adults who are at low risk of complications from vaccination and sick adults and all children, sick or well, who are at far greater risk of vaccine complications. Nor has CDC promoted the wide use of the semipermeable membrane dressing, which greatly decreases the risk of accidental vaccination of others. Finally, the ease of control after an event, particularly the value of vaccinating after exposure to smallpox, has been both overstated and misstated.

Result: The perception of vaccine risk by many medical and public health practitioners, as well as by the public, is far greater than the actual risk. Misperceptions remain about the spread and control of smallpox after a bioterrorism event. . . .

In clearing up continuing misperceptions, the following points are of particular importance:

1. Transmission of smallpox is very possible and should be assumed before the appearance of any visible rash.
2. In a bioterrorism outbreak states should plan to move to local mass vaccination as they also identify and vaccinate easily identified contacts of the first case or cases.
3. Vaccination after exposure, particularly within three to five days, is likely to prevent death but is unlikely to prevent disease and further spread of smallpox. Therefore, though valuable for individuals, it has limited value in planning for post-event control in the general population.
4. Fast and effective post-event control is critically dependant upon completing substantial pre-event vaccination as called for in Phase II of the president's plan. . . .

Why post-event vaccination is flawed

Smallpox expert Dr. D.A. Henderson warned as early as 1999 that malicious dissemination of smallpox by bioterrorists could be disastrous. There is much to support his opinion, and it is not unreasonable to conclude that this risk is the primary rationale behind the president's plan. However, there are powerful voices that still say smallpox is difficult to transmit and maintain that the lessons of control from the eradication years are valid today.

It is essential to recognize that eradication took place over a period of more than 10 years when the level of population immunity was growing, populations were far less mobile than today, and there was no malicious intent to disseminate smallpox. . . . Because the speed of post-event vaccination is directly dependent on the number of vaccinators willing to expose themselves to the risk of smallpox, the smaller the number of immunized vaccinators, the faster smallpox would spread across the country. Further, if neither health care workers nor the general population are immunized, our hospitals and medical care system will be at grave risk of being swamped and losing significant capacity after a smallpox attack. That is exactly what the president's plan was designed to prevent. . . .

We have enough vaccine to vaccinate the entire country in case of an attack. But instead of vaccinating rapidly within 10 days, with our current level of preparedness, we could easily take one to two months, with needless spread of disease, avoidable deaths, and much suffering and economic loss. We can muddle through. But muddling through at the expense of hundreds, perhaps thousands, of lives is not good enough. . . .

Fast and effective post-event control is critically dependant upon completing substantial pre-event vaccination.

The [2003] letter to the director of CDC from the Institute of Medicine's Committee on Smallpox Vaccination Program Implementation [reads in part:]

". . . a high level of preparedness may well be possible without vaccinating any personnel pre-event" is wrong, irresponsible, and dangerous. In another part of their letter, the committee suggests that individual states may have goals of vaccinating their populations in 2 to 10 days. The impossibility of achieving either with no pre-event vaccination is not mentioned. Later, the committee says, "It is unclear . . . how numbers of vaccinated personnel relate to the ability to respond effectively to a smallpox attack." These and other inconsistencies and contradictions are obvious yet not addressed by the committee. In yet another place the committee suggests that in a post-event situation it may not be possible to immediately vaccinate everyone, so plans should be made for "prioritizing categories of vaccinees . . . pre-event" or rationing access. We can only speculate about the problems of crowd control when access to vaccine is needlessly denied in the face of a disease with a 30 percent fatality rate. Although the committee mentioned the military have vaccinated over 450,000 people, they failed to comment on the fundamental finding from the military experience that smallpox is a safe vaccine when administered with care to healthy adults. In brief, the IOM letter illustrates poor risk assessment and inadequate systems thinking that neither serve good public health nor support sound national preparation for a possible terrorist release of smallpox. . . .

Rapid post-event control

With sufficient vaccine and VIG, the nation now has the material, but not the human, capacity to rapidly control a bioterrorist smallpox outbreak. Pre-event vaccination of 10,000,000 medical, public health, and emergency workers is central and essential for rapid post-event control.

However, few health and emergency workers have opted for voluntary vaccination. The overt reasons are

- inadequate and misleading vaccine risk information provided by CDC,
- delay in passing liability and compensation legislation, and
- insufficient education about and support for vaccination by key leaders in the administration directed to the public and key professional groups.

Further, a variety of subtle but powerful underlying reasons is delaying vaccination and weakening post-event planning. Perhaps the most important are deficient systems thinking in public health and a public health culture that prefers to be reactive rather than proactive.

In the near term, far better information about the risk of vaccination along with a clear rationale for the president's plan are needed. With the passage of compensation legislation, the administration now needs to reemphasize that vaccination is safe and that our nation's security requires the timely completion of the national pre-event plan. Those actions will effectively neutralize the weapons potential of smallpox.

12

The Smallpox Threat Does Not Warrant Mass Vaccination

Henry I. Miller

Henry I. Miller, a physician, is a fellow at the Hoover Institution in Stanford, California, and the author of America's Health: A Proposal to Reform the Food and Drug Administration. *He was an official at the Food and Drug Administration (FDA) from 1979 to 1994.*

Although a majority of Americans would voluntarily undergo smallpox vaccination if it were offered, recent research shows that the vaccine is more dangerous than previously predicted. In fact, the smallpox vaccine will provoke serious side effects in thirteen hundred of every 1 million recipients. This risk is all the more unjustified considering that smallpox no longer exists in nature. Moreover, the threat of a bioterrorist attack aimed at infecting the U.S. population with smallpox has been exaggerated; acquiring, cultivating, and disseminating the virus, which exists only in government storage facilities, would be difficult. Limited vaccination of medical personnel and government first responders is a more prudent policy than mass vaccination of the American adult population.

Sixty-one percent of Americans would opt for smallpox immunization if the vaccine were available, according to a nationwide survey [in late 2002] by the Harvard School of Public Health. However, the vaccine has long been known to be dangerous, and the most recent data suggest that it is even more hazardous than previously predicted.

This is a prescription for bad medicine.

Medically and epidemiologically, smallpox is the most feared and potentially devastating of all infectious agents. Far more contagious than SARS [severe acute respiratory syndrome], for example, it spreads readily from person to person via droplets coughed up by infected persons, through direct contact, and from contaminated clothing and bed linens. Smallpox is fatal in approximately one-third of previously unvaccinated persons who contract the disease, compared to four to six percent for SARS, and 0.1 percent for hepatitis A and B.

The [George W.] Bush administration, Congress and the media have raised the specter of terrorists using smallpox virus as a weapon, and the government has obtained sufficient vaccine for every man, woman and child in this country. (Routine smallpox vaccinations ceased here in 1972.) The administration has begun to vaccinate 500,000 health care workers, and has announced that the vaccine will eventually be made available to the population at large.

The vaccine is not safe

But the vaccine may be more of a threat to public health than smallpox itself.

The vaccine consists of live vaccinia virus, a close relative of smallpox. Highly impure and crude by the modern standards of gene-spliced vaccines such as those that have been successfully deployed against hepatitis B since the 1980s, the vaccine is not much improved from the one introduced by the English physician Edward Jenner in the eighteenth century.

During its use in the decades before 1972, smallpox vaccine was known to provoke various serious side effects, including rashes; spread from the inoculation site to face, eyelid, mouth or genitalia; and generalized infection. The data suggested that of every million vaccinees, approximately 1,000 in a million would experience serious side effects, 15 of which would be life-threatening; three would develop encephalitis, which can lead to permanent neurological damage; and between one and three would die. People whose immune systems were suppressed, or who had ever had eczema, were at the highest risk of side effects.

The vaccine may be more of a threat to public health than smallpox itself.

Data released [in 2003] by the CDC [Centers for Disease Control and Prevention] suggest that the 30-plus-year-old vaccine may be even more dangerous now. Of the approximately 33,400 health care workers who have received the vaccine, 45 have experienced serious side effects. Extrapolated, that means that of every million vaccinees, we would expect to see more than 1,300 serious side effects. So if the 61 percent of the eligible population who say they want the vaccine were to get it, we would expect about 165,000 serious side effects, and 250 to 300 deaths. (To put this into perspective, as of May 5, [2003], SARS had caused 61 illnesses and no fatalities in the United States.)

The CDC has also revealed that 103 expectant mothers received the smallpox vaccine, even after being warned about possible dangerous side effects. This is alarming because the vaccine can cause an infection known as fetal vaccinia, which can kill the unborn or newborn baby, or cause premature birth.

Worse still, the CDC's findings disclose completely new kinds of adverse effects: Ten persons have experienced myopericarditis, an inflammation of the heart muscle or the sac that surrounds the heart, and six have had heart attacks after being vaccinated.

Perhaps it is not surprising that the decades-old vaccine is more dangerous to today's population: Americans are older, and more are immunosuppressed as a result of HIV infections, cancer chemotherapy, organ transplants and steroid treatment. Even a small increase in the rate of side effects or mortality becomes significant when multiplied by hundreds of millions.

The vaccine interferes with other medical procedures

There are other problems with widespread vaccination besides the inevitable morbidity and mortality directly attributable to the vaccine. First, blood banks will not accept blood from persons for at least several weeks following vaccination or infection from exposure to a vaccinee.

> *It is imprudent to inoculate widely against a non-existent disease with a vaccine that has serious and frequent side effects.*

Second, it is unclear who will bear the financial liability for damage to vaccinees, or to persons secondarily infected by exposure to vaccinees. (The Bush administration's remedy was to propose a scheme for compensating persons injured by smallpox vaccination. However, it does not define rigorously and scientifically the circumstances and timeframes of injuries that are likely to be related to the vaccine; and without these scientific definitions, the administration's plan creates yet another open-ended federal entitlement program—the last thing we need at a time of skyrocketing health care costs and federal deficits.)

Third, persons who receive the smallpox vaccine will develop a long-term immunity that will interfere with poxvirus-based treatments now being developed against HIV and various cancers.

We are being penalized once again by the law of unintended consequences.

A smallpox outbreak is highly unlikely

If re-emergence of smallpox were likely, widespread vaccination would be appropriate. However, smallpox virus no longer occurs in nature but is limited to two known, legitimate repositories, one in the United States, the other in Russia (and perhaps to illegitimate ones in several other countries). It is very difficult to obtain, and to cultivate and disseminate.

Also, smallpox is not immediately contagious after infection. It can be transmitted from one person to another only after an incubation period and the appearance of the characteristic rash, by which time the victim is prostrate, bedridden and probably hospitalized. Therefore, the much-publicized scenario in which suicide terrorists infect themselves and then spread the disease widely through the population is not a realistic one.

Moreover, although universal smallpox vaccination was phased out throughout the world during the 1970s, individuals who were vaccinated prior to that time retain significant immunity from these immunizations, both against contracting the disease and against a fatal outcome in case of infection. Scientists know a great deal about the long-term retention of immunity from a landmark study of 1,163 smallpox cases in Liverpool, England in 1902–1903. Among those infected, seven percent of the people 50 or older who had received the vaccine as children experienced severe disease and death, while 26 percent of unvaccinated people in that age group contracted serious cases of smallpox and all died.

Limited vaccination is adequate

Even if an outbreak were to occur, public health authorities know how to respond. Control depends upon early detection, quarantine of infected individuals, surveillance of contacts, and focused, aggressive vaccination of all possible contacts—an approach dubbed "quarantine-ring vaccination."

Finally, the federal government has taken steps to cope with the possibility of a terrorist attack involving smallpox, by educating doctors to recognize the disease and by vaccinating small teams of experts who can rush to any part of the country to confirm the diagnosis, and contain and treat an outbreak. One important lesson that SARS has taught us is the importance of a rapid, well-coordinated, and systematic response to outbreaks of serious infectious diseases.

It is imprudent to inoculate widely against a non-existent disease with a vaccine that has serious and frequent side effects. Better to immunize only a minimum of government first-responders and hospital workers who would be involved in a reported outbreak, then vaccinate more widely if an actual case is found. Any other course of action would be driven more by public relations than public health.

Sherlock Holmes admonished in *A Scandal in Bohemia* that "it is a capital mistake to theorize before one has data." It is worse to make the wrong decision after one has data.

13

Global Public Health Systems Must Be Improved to Combat Infectious Diseases

David L. Heymann

David L. Heymann is executive director of communicable disease programs at the World Health Organization (WHO), a specialized agency of the United Nations whose goal is to achieve the optimum health of all peoples. Among its core functions is promoting the development and testing of new technologies and programs aimed at global disease control and risk reduction.

The threat of infectious diseases is global in scope, so the responses of the public health infrastructure must be global, too, and aimed at prevention. Important aspects of disease control include timely surveillance to track outbreaks and rapid response capabilities. Also vital are partnerships between public and private-sector agencies. The three-pronged approach taken by the World Health Organization to combat infectious diseases involves containing known risks, responding to the unexpected, and improving preparedness.

Editor's note: The following viewpoint was originally given as testimony before the U.S. Senate Committee on Foreign Relations, Hearing on the Threat of Bioterrorism and the Spread of Infectious Diseases, on September 5, 2001.

The world now finds itself in a situation where epidemics are again spreading around the globe unchecked, but this time at unprecedented speed. New or newly recognized diseases are being reported at the rate of approximately one per year. AIDS emerged as an important infectious disease in the early 1980s and is now entrenched on a scale that threatens global security. Other emerging diseases, such as Ebola haemorrhagic fever

David L. Heymann, statement before the U.S. Senate Committee on Foreign Relations, Hearing on the Threat of Bioterrorism and the Spread of Infectious Diseases, September 5, 2001.

and new variant Creutzfeld-Jakob disease, illustrate the severe damage caused by lethal new agents that cannot currently be curbed by vaccines or drugs. In 1997 and 1999, when influenza viruses previously confined, respectively, to birds and swine suddenly appeared in humans, experts voiced fears of a pandemic on the scale of the deadly Spanish Flu of 1918, which some believe was caused by an avian virus that first crossed the species barrier to swine before jumping to humans. Altogether, over 30 new infectious diseases have emerged over the past 25 years. . . .

Apart from the need to cope with the emergence and spread of new diseases, public health infrastructures are further burdened by the dramatic resurgence of older epidemic-prone diseases such as malaria, dengue, tuberculosis, cholera, and yellow fever. Cholera, for example, is now causing epidemics in parts of Latin America where it had previously been quiescent for over 100 years. The global spread of dengue, which began in Southeast Asia in the 1950s, has intensified dramatically, showing a four-fold increase with unprecedented numbers of its deadly haemorrhagic form. On 23 August 2001, Venezuela's president declared the country's current dengue epidemic, with more than double the number of cases seen in the previous year and over 600 cases of its potentially lethal form, a national emergency. . . .

The need for global solutions

Taken together, the threats posed by emerging and re-emerging infectious diseases, and by the emergence and spread of antimicrobial resistance are serious, steadily growing, and universally costly. Their nature is inherently global, with causes related to the world's growing interconnectedness, and with consequences that must be addressed by global solutions, ideally aimed at prevention.

As an international health agency with over 50 years of experience, the World Health Organization [WHO] is well placed to gather global disease intelligence and coordinate the rapid, multifaceted response needed to contain outbreaks quickly and prevent their international spread. . . .

> *Public health infrastructures are . . . burdened by the dramatic resurgence of older epidemic-prone diseases such as malaria, dengue, tuberculosis, cholera, and yellow fever.*

WHO coordinates a large number of electronic "detective" systems and databases for keeping experts alert to changes in the volatile infectious disease situation. These networks, most of which now operate in real time, keep watch over disease-related events ranging from new strains of influenza virus, through outbreaks of salmonellosis and dengue, to the emergence of drug-resistant pathogens. Most of these networks also include quality assurance and training components to ensure that data submitted from all parts of the world are comparable and conform to established standards. The oldest of these, FluNet, was established over 50 years ago and has served as the prototype for the design and implementation of subsequent systems. It now draws support from 110 collaborating laboratories in 84 countries. The sensitivity of FluNet has recently proved vital in the early detection of cases where influenza virus strains have crossed the species barrier from animals, such as swine and poultry, to infect humans.

These surveillance networks all operate within the framework of the International Health Regulations, which provide the only international legally-binding instrument, implemented by WHO, governing the reporting of epidemic-prone diseases and the application of measures to prevent their spread. . . .

The framework for disease surveillance and response: a three-pronged approach

The framework for global disease surveillance and response is based on the use of a large number of partners, including government agencies, nongovernmental organizations, the private sector, and industry. Such partnerships allow WHO to magnify the impact of its efforts considerably.

The framework relies on a three-pronged approach, with different strategies for combatting known risks and unexpected events, and for improving both global and national preparedness.

Containing known risks. Epidemic-prone diseases, such as cholera, dengue, influenza, measles, meningitis, shigellosis, and yellow fever, and foodborne diseases pose a constant threat to human populations. They are well adapted to transmission in human populations either directly from person to person, through transmission by insects and other disease vectors, or by contamination of the environment or food. These diseases are generally well understood and, in most cases, effective measures are available for their control.

WHO maintains numerous programmes for the monitoring and control of these well-known and almost constant risks to public health. Disease-specific networks of partners help WHO mount a rapid response when outbreaks occur, at times following a breakdown in standard public health control measures in the country concerned. Established protocols, based on extensive experience, facilitate prompt, coordinated action. For some of these infections, such as epidemic meningitis, influenza, and yellow fever, WHO also collaborates with researchers and industry to anticipate future outbreaks and ensure that adequate emergency vaccine supplies are available when needed. Other known risks monitored by WHO include those caused by foodborne diseases and the emergence and spread of drug resistance.

Responding to the unexpected. . . . WHO has recently established innovative mechanisms for responding to previously unknown diseases and unexpected or unusual disease events. These mechanisms take full advantage of the powerful new opportunities for heightened vigilance and rapid response that have been created by the widespread use of electronic communications. To heighten vigilance, WHO takes advantage of a semi-automatic electronic system, developed for WHO by Health Canada, that continuously and systematically crawls Web sites, news wires, public health email services, electronic discussion groups, including the US-based Pro-MED, and local online newspapers for rumours of outbreaks. In this way, WHO is able to scan the world for informal news that gives cause for suspecting an unusual disease event. A WHO team responsible for outbreak verification investigates suspicious reports each morning to determine whether they pose a threat of international health concern. When appropriate, WHO uses its technical and geographical resources to verify the presence of an outbreak. Since 1998, WHO has used this system to verify over 800 outbreaks of potential international importance.

To ensure that heightened vigilance is accompanied by a rapid response, WHO enlarged and formalized its procedures for outbreak detection, verification, and response in April 2000, when the Global Outbreak Alert and Response Network was formed. The Network draws together 72 existing networks, many operating under WHO's responsibility, others maintained by national governments or regional nongovernmental organizations. The Network reports and verifies information, on a daily basis, from a wide range of formal sources, including ministries of health, national institutes of public health, government and military health facilities and laboratories, and nongovernmental organizations, such as the Red Cross, having a strong presence in epidemic-prone countries. When an outbreak is judged to require international assistance, as agreed upon in confidential consultation with the affected country and with experts in the Network, WHO uses the latest electronic communication tools to coordinate quick and appropriate assistance. Since early 2000, the network has launched effective international responses in Afghanistan, Bangladesh, Egypt, Ethiopia, Kosovo, Saudi Arabia, Sierra Leone, Sudan, Uganda, and Yemen.

The framework for global disease surveillance and response is based on the use of . . . government agencies, non-governmental organizations, the private sector, and industry.

The work of coordinating large-scale international assistance, which can involve many agencies from many nations, is facilitated by operational protocols, developed by WHO, which set out standardized procedures for the alert and verification process, communications, coordination of the response, emergency evacuation, research, evaluation, monitoring, and relations with the media. WHO has also issued guidelines for the behaviour of foreign nationals during and after field operations in the host country. By setting out a chain of command, and imposing order on the containment response, such protocols help protect against the very real risk that samples of a lethal pathogen might be collected for later provision to a terrorist group.

Improving preparedness. WHO conducts a number of activities aimed at helping countries strengthen their laboratory and epidemiological capacity and take advantage of new tools such as HealthMap (an interactive information and mapping system), and remote sensing data from NASA [National Aeronautics and Space Administration] and other satellites. WHO suppors the Training Programmes in Epidemiology and Public Health Interventions network (TEPHINET), another global network utilized by the Global Outbreak Alert and Response Network, which seeks, through shared resources and expertise, to enhance the effectiveness of national training programmes. In February 2001, WHO opened a new office in Lyon, France, to provide two-year specialized training for epidemiologists and laboratory specialists from developing countries where the epidemic risk is greatest. The training, which includes a six-week course in Lyon, is followed by specially tailored field work and support in the home country, supervised by Lyon-based staff. In so doing, the new programme is working to strengthen disease detection and response activities in those countries where epidemics and unexpected disease events are most likely to occur.

As another example, a working group on long-term preparedness for outbreak response was recently established to help ensure that the energy and resources that are provided to a country for the investigation and containment of an outbreak do not vanish after containment, but are instead harnessed in the form of long-term technical assistance. During 1998 and 1999 major epidemics, including outbreaks of haemorrhagic fever, cholera, and meningitis, caused a significant increase in morbidity and mortality in southern Sudan and necessitated major international assistance. In 1999, a WHO-coordinated international team responding to an outbreak of relapsing fever set up an Early Warning and Response Network (EWARN) in partnership with nongovernmental organizations present in the field. With support from several sources, EWARN has been expanded to cover seven diseases and a wide geographical area, and now ensures that epidemics are rapidly detected and investigated while responses are launched quickly using prepositioned materials. This international partnership in the field has already saved thousands of lives and is sustained by systematic capacity building among the local communities.

Capacity building for national epidemic detection and response is far more cost-effective than mounting an international response. During the Ebola outbreak in Uganda, containment activities left behind permanent improvements in the form of isolation wards at two hospitals in Gulu district, a community-based early warning surveillance and response system for priority infectious diseases, and sustained improvements in civil administration through the establishment of a community registry of births and deaths. In June 2001, a new focus of three suspected cases of haemorrhagic fever was detected by local staff within three days of onset, patients were immediately isolated in the recently established ward, and specimens were despatched for testing at the WHO Collaborating Centre in South Africa, where results fortunately proved negative. In this case, strengthened national capacity made it possible to defend global health security through local vigilance, without the need for costly international assistance. . . .

Preparedness for a bioterrorist attack

In view of the devastating impact on civilian populations that use of [biological] weapons could have, [WHO] urges governments to prepare response plans as an integral part of existing national emergency plans. The strengthening of public health infrastructure, particularly for surveillance and response, is singled out as a major contribution to preparedness. The establishment of routine, sensitive, and near real time disease surveillance systems enhances preparedness for deliberate as well as natural outbreaks. National systems are important as experience has shown that many region-wide and global systems are inadequately sensitive to pick up local outbreaks quickly.

Strengthening . . . public health infrastructures represents one of the surest, most sustainable, and most cost-effective measures for preventing the international spread of diseases.

National surveillance systems need to be in place well in advance of possible intentional use of a biological weapon, as adequate data on the prevalence of background diseases are needed to aid recognition of an unusual and possibly deliberately caused disease. Moreover, the epidemiological techniques needed to investigate deliberate and natural outbreaks are the same. Since many of the agents that can be used as bioweapons cause disease in animals, countries also need to establish mechanisms for the routine exchange of information between the public health and veterinary sectors.

Within the context of its outbreak alert and response activities, WHO has developed protocols for containing outbreaks of diseases, such as anthrax and viral haemorrhagic fevers, which could result from the intentional use of biological agents. As part of its official mandate for dealing with smallpox-related issues in the post-eradication era, WHO is responsible for ensuring the security of the remaining stocks of smallpox virus and overseeing their final fate.

Traditionally, one of the main factors undermining the effectiveness of infectious disease surveillance has been the reluctance of countries to report outbreaks due to fear of the negative impact this news would have on travel, trade, and tourism. This traditional reluctance is now beginning to change. In line with the growth of electronic media, approximately 65% of the world's first news about infectious disease events during the past four years has come not from official country notifications but from informal sources, including press reports and the Internet. Transparency about outbreaks and prompt reporting have therefore become increasingly important: unverified rumours of an outbreak or unusual disease can have a negative impact on travel and trade in the country and its neighbours even though the rumour may be totally unjustified or grossly exaggerated.

In May 2001, the World Health Assembly, the supreme governing body of WHO, adopted by consensus a resolution on global health security that considerably strengthens WHO's capacity to act in response to outbreaks and epidemics. WHO is now in a position to investigate and verify rumoured outbreaks even prior to receipt of an official notification from the government of the country concerned. Though WHO continues to confer, in confidence, with governments and secure their agreement to mount an international response, this strengthened capacity allows WHO to act with unprecedented speed.

In the new order of the electronic era, countries are increasingly aware of the advantages of prompt outbreak reporting and official verification, accompanied by prompt international aid when needed, and prompt advice from WHO to the international community concerning the associated risks and the realistic need for restrictions on travel and trade. For example, during the Ebola outbreak in Uganda, WHO was informed as soon as the first suspected cases were detected, and a WHO-coordinated investigative team was on the spot within 24 hours. Throughout the five-month long epidemic, WHO issued 42 updated reports on the epidemic via its Web site. The country's borders were never closed.

During the May debate that preceded adoption of the resolution on global health security, delegations from developing countries repeatedly urged WHO to help them strengthen the laboratory and epidemiological capacities needed to detect outbreaks quickly, identify their cause, monitor their spread, and introduce containment measures. Both the need to act and the will to do so are present. The risks are known, immediate, alarming, and relevant to every country in the world. WHO and its many partners and member states know what needs to be done.

Mechanisms for monitoring and containing these risks exist, but need to be strengthened. Above all, the multiple threats posed by infectious diseases—whether well known or unexpected—have global causes and consequences that can only be addressed through global solutions. Strengthening of national capacities and public health infrastructures represents one of the surest, most sustainable, and most cost-effective measures for preventing the international spread of diseases and thus defending global health security for the benefit of all.

14

Vaccine Development Is Vital to Controlling Infectious Diseases

Gustav Nossal

Gustav Nossal is professor emeritus of the University of Melbourne. He chairs the Strategic Advisory Council of the Bill and Melinda Gates Children's Vaccine Program and the Strategic Advisory Group of Experts of the World Health Organization's Vaccines and Biologicals Program.

Vaccines have been dramatically successful in combating smallpox and polio during the twentieth century, and continuing vaccine development promises to be a key factor in the control of infectious diseases in the twenty-first century. No other treatment is as cost-effective. After smallpox was eradicated in the late 1970s, the focus of vaccination shifted to childhood immunization programs, which have been quite effective against diphtheria, pertussis, tetanus, polio, measles and tuberculosis. In poor countries today, however, the infant immunization rate averages just over 50 percent, an unacceptably low coverage. The three diseases for which vaccines are most needed are AIDS, malaria, and tuberculosis.

It took 181 years from Edward Jenner's introduction of a smallpox vaccine for public health efforts to succeed in eradicating that disease from the globe. Even today, the gap between the introduction of a vaccine in the industrialized countries and its use in the poorer nations remains dauntingly long. Yet vaccines have proven themselves to be the most cost-effective public health tools in history.

How will progress in vaccines affect public health in the next 100 years? What lingering diseases will they help us conquer? How will their global use be financed? What lessons from experience can be applied to future vaccination campaigns?

If one had a crystal ball to look at the future of vaccines, it would no doubt reveal some important and heartening milestones, possibly including the following:

Gustav Nossal, "Protecting Our Progeny: The Future of Vaccines," *Perspectives in Health*, vol. 7, 2002.

- By 2005, significant progress toward if not achievement of the global eradication of polio
- By 2010, vaccines against meningitis, pneumonia, rotavirus-caused diarrhea and human papilloma virus (the cause of cervical cancer)
- By 2015, vaccines against AIDS, malaria and pulmonary tuberculosis, and the global control of measles
- By 2025, the ability to protect infants against at least 20 pathogens throughout their lives

In reality, we can only speculate meaningfully on the future by thoroughly analyzing the past and present. Yet even in that real-life context, the prospects look bright indeed for a major impact of vaccines on global human health.

Infant immunization programs

Smallpox is an important and encouraging case study. Though the vaccine has been around for more than two centuries, it took a mere 11 years for a disciplined campaign that was adequately financed and brilliantly led to achieve eradication. What came as an encore?

Just as smallpox was nearing eradication in the late 1970s, the World Health Organization (WHO) launched the Expanded Programme on Immunization (EPI), which included six infant vaccines: against diphtheria, pertussis, tetanus, poliomyelitis, measles and tuberculosis. Although EPI got off to a slow start, the concept of universal childhood immunization was embraced seriously from 1984 on.

As a result, global immunization of infants rose progressively to just under 80 percent coverage by 1990. This overall statistic, however, hides the fact that coverage was quite uneven. In countries with per capita GDP [gross domestic product] of less than $1,000, coverage reached a mean of just over 50 percent. In the Americas, coverage was much better (often spectacularly) than the global average.

Unfortunately, since 1990 no real further progress has occurred, and indeed coverage has slipped in a number of countries, with coverage in the poorest countries now at just over 40 percent. EPI has saved many millions of lives and must be counted as a success. Yet globally there are still at least 2 million vaccine-preventable deaths every year in children under 5.

Polio eradication

With the Americas once again in the lead, global polio eradication efforts began in earnest in 1988. It was soon realized that routine infant immunization, although essential, could not do the job alone. It was buttressed by three additional strategies: national immunization days (NID), a global system for surveillance, and "mop-up" operations, that is, intense vaccination efforts around the last few index cases.

National Immunization Days represented a huge effort in social mobilization, receiving extraordinary help from Rotary International, the news media, the government sector and, particularly, highly involved health ministries. On a single day, all of a country's children under 5 were lined up and given the oral Sabin vaccine. This succeeded in finding many hard-to-reach children who, for one reason or another, had not been caught in the routine immunization net.

As it turned out, it was necessary to have two NID a month apart, and to repeat the effort yearly for at least three years, turning Rotary's Polio Plus campaign into a monumental task. As polio gradually came under control, it became important to detect the residual cases. Therefore, a surveillance system was instituted to bring all cases of acute paralysis (technically termed flaccid to distinguish them from strokes) to the notice of health authorities. When cases were found, two stool samples were sent to accredited laboratories to see if the polio virus could be grown. This tedious but vital surveillance task has been absolutely crucial.

Finally, "mop-up" operations, consisting of dwelling-to-dwelling immunization around the last known cases, are the last step toward eradication. Thanks to this quadruple strategy, there have been no indigenous wild polio cases in the Western Hemisphere since 1991, none in the Western Pacific Region since 1997, and none in the European Region since 1998. Even in India, wild polio is now essentially confined to two northern states.

Vaccines have proven themselves to be the most cost-effective public health tools in history.

[Until 2005] WHO will be concentrating on 10 countries in Africa and South Asia, five of which are conflict ridden and five others "reservoir countries" because of high population density and very poor living standards. The target year for the global eradication of the wild polio virus is 2005.

Although the Polio Plus campaign is a vertical program (as opposed to horizontal programs, which seek to provide primary health care across a broad front), it has broader implications. First, in many cases vitamin A supplements are administered simultaneously. Second, it provides a contact point between remote and disadvantaged rural poor and national health systems, often leading to a greater awareness of other available health interventions.

Global alliance

The experiences of both smallpox and polio show the extraordinary power of the vaccine approach. But what about the present state of play? In 1998, there was a sense that new energies were needed in global immunization efforts. Donor interest in EPI was fading, the vaccine infrastructure in many countries was deteriorating, and research was lagging on new vaccines for diseases occurring only in poor countries.

But as WHO, UNICEF [the United Nations Children's Fund], the World Bank and leading academics were searching for a new dynamic, help came from an unexpected source: William H. Gates III and his wife, Melinda French Gates. The Gates Foundation made an initial pledge of $100 million to a Children's Vaccine Program, at first designed to determine and overcome the chief roadblocks to the introduction of important new vaccines into the EPI. Within two years, the Gates' extraordinary generosity had led to a total of $1.4 billion committed to vaccine-related projects, including considerable research and development funds and a $750 million gift earmarked for a Global Fund for Children's Vaccines, administered by UNICEF. The Vaccine Fund, as it is now known, targets the 74 poorest countries in the world, namely, those with per capita GDP of less than $1,000 per annum. Several countries have added pledges to the fund, and it now stands at more than $1 billion.

The experiences of both smallpox and polio show the extraordinary power of the vaccine approach.

After extensive consultation with all stakeholders, the Global Alliance for Vaccines and Immunization (GAVI) was launched in 2000 as an unincorporated alliance of WHO, UNICEF, the World Bank, the Gates and Rockefeller foundations, and other nongovernmental organizations, along with bilateral donors, developing country health authorities and vaccine manufacturers from both developed and developing countries. . . .

GAVI has set itself three major goals. The first is to improve infrastructure for immunization in countries where it is inferior through cash grants dependent on a demonstrable increase in vaccination coverage.

The second is to purchase, for selected countries, vaccines beyond the traditional six, primarily hepatitis B, yellow fever and Hemophilus influenzae B, or Hib, for meningitis, pneumonia and septicemia.

The third and longer-term goal is to do applied research and development work for newer vaccines already well down the track, such as against pneumococcus and rotavirus. Already two-thirds of GAVI s target countries have grants and/or vaccine supplies flowing to them. Yet sustainability is a real worry, as the beneficiary countries will gradually have to subsume the costs of the vaccines into their own health budgets.

Future vaccines

Despite the amazing progress of immunological science, there are many diseases for which we do not yet have an effective vaccine. We could see rapid progress in the so-called "low-hanging fruit," those vaccines-in-research whose underlying principles have largely been established and that seem to require relatively straightforward development work to become available. This is probably the case for the A subtype of meningococcus, responsible for horrible meningitis epidemics in sub-Saharan Africa; for rotavirus, an important cause of infantile diarrhea; and for pneumococcus, which will involve major expense because each of many different disease-causing types will need to be included in an eventual vaccine.

It would be surprising if vaccines for these pathogens were not available within five to seven years. Again, we must seek public sector funds for their early introduction.

Somewhat more speculative are vaccines against shigellosis, or bacillary dysentery, a cause of some 800,000 deaths per year, nearly all in very poor countries; and against *Helicobacter pylori*, the cause of peptic ulcer disease, chronic gastritis and a big proportion of gastric cancers. It is doubtful whether the pharmaceutical industry will come up with sufficient research funding to drive these vaccines all the way to registration. The chances are better for a vaccine against human papilloma virus (HPV), the cause of cervical cancer and genital warts, because industrialized countries have a major interest in preventing these problems.

From a public health viewpoint, there are three "future vaccines" of even greater interest: those against HIV/AIDS, malaria and tuberculosis. These are so important that each deserves some discussion. So far, an AIDS vaccine has eluded us, primarily because the human immunodeficiency virus has such devilishly clever tricks up its sleeve to foil the host's natural defense system. It chooses to live in and destroy one of the most important cells of the immune system, the so-called CD4+, or helper T cell. It also infects scavenger cells important in initiating immune responses. It can go underground in these cells, only to emerge much later. Being an RNA (ribonucleic acid) virus, it is subject to a very high rate of mutation, so that when the immune system does manage to polish off most of the virus, a mutant form with a different antigenic signature pops up, needing to be dealt with in turn. Finally, the active recognition sites on the grappling hooks that the virus uses to hang onto its target cell are skillfully hidden from the prying eyes of antibody molecules until the very moment of docking and entry.

It would be surprising if vaccines for [meningococcus, rotavirus, and pneumococcus] were not available within five to seven years.

Despite these challenges, progress is being made toward a vaccine. Stratagems have been devised to evoke antibodies that are broadly active against different subtypes of the virus. During the long latent period of the disease, while the patient is still well, the body's killer T cells do fight against the virus, keeping the total load in the body relatively low. If a vaccine can provoke those T cells into intense activity before infection occurs, the very small virus load entering the body might be destroyed completely.

We have good ideas about how to craft such a vaccine; it is now necessary to trial these one by one in the clinic, a process that is necessarily very slow. An alliance known as the International AIDS Vaccine Initiative (IAVI) has raised sizable funds to speed clinical trials, so that several different vaccine candidates can be assessed simultaneously. Much of this trial work will have to be conducted in developing countries, given their higher incidence of infection.

Targeting malaria

Malaria is the worst of the human parasitic diseases, killing between 1 million and 2 million people every year, chiefly in Africa. People living in endemic areas eventually develop partial immunity, such that they do not get attacks despite having parasites in their blood. If they move to a non-malarial area for several years, they gradually lose their immunity.

Here, scientists will have to do better than nature.

There are four susceptible points in the parasite's life cycle when it may be vulnerable. First, a motile form known as a sporozoite is introduced into the skin by the night-feeding female Anopheles mosquito. Within less than half an hour, sporozoites reach and enter liver cells. Up to that point, antibodies directed to the sporozoite surface might lead to their destruction. Once in the liver, the parasite multiplies, during the process shedding bits that will reach the surface of the cell. If a killer T cell recognizes these bits (called peptides or T cell epitopes), the affected liver cell is attacked and destroyed before it can release its progeny into the bloodstream. Infection is thus aborted.

From a public health viewpoint, there are three "future vaccines" of [greatest] interest: those against HIV/AIDS, malaria and tuberculosis.

But once the progeny (known as merozoites) are in the blood, they quickly attach to and infect red blood cells. They then multiply, rupture the red cell, and enter a new one. It is this blood-stage cycle that is responsible for the symptoms of the disease. In its transit from one red cell to the next, the merozoite is briefly susceptible to antibody.

Finally, some merozoite-infected red cells release gametocytes, sexual forms of the parasite, which can mature within the mosquito into male and female gametes. When these unite, the life cycle is completed. If one were to make antibodies to these gametocytes, one would not help the patient, but at a population level, transmission would be blocked, and eventually the disease might be brought under control.

Experimental vaccines incorporating each of these four sets of ideas have been shown to work in model systems. It is now a question of subjecting them to phased human trials. One of the many Gates Foundation programs, the Malaria Vaccine Initiative, is planning to do just that. So far, some partial success has been achieved in human trials with a sporozoite vaccine and a combination blood-stage antigen vaccine.

Attacking TB

Why do we need a tuberculosis vaccine other than the BCG (Bacillus Calmette-Guerin) vaccine? Simply because this live, attenuated bacterium can protect infants from tuberculosis but appears incapable of coping with the real problem, namely, pulmonary tuberculosis in adolescents and young adults. Though not as far advanced as it is for AIDS and malaria, research toward a new TB vaccine is exploring plenty of bright ideas, including both live attenuated and molecular approaches. A recently completed tubercle bacillus genome project is speeding the search. One of the biggest problems, not only with the "big three" but also with other vaccines, is the fact that pure protein molecules made by genetic engineering do not by themselves induce a strong immune response. For this we need immune-strengthening substances called adjuvants. Many are under development, but these tend to be toxic, and the search for more satisfactory adjuvants is intense.

Alternatively, we need new and craftier ways of delivering the vaccine. For example, we can take the gene for an important vaccine molecule (or antigen) and transplant it into a virus, then inject that virus, which will strongly alert the immune system. We can also inject DNA coding for antigens, which enters cells and then creates a factory where the body itself is manufacturing vaccine molecules over a considerable period. One highly promising strategy is known as prime-boost, in which a DNA vaccine is injected first and an engineered virus next. This has worked well in animal models of both HIV/AIDS and malaria.

Genomics has opened up other entirely new avenues as well. Plants can be engineered to produce antigens, so an edible vaccine is feasible. This would have to be constructed so that either a mucosal adjuvant or some other immune-enhancing factor was also present. Vaccines can also be applied to the skin and, amazingly, find their way into the body, yielding a transdermal vaccine. Here again, immune enhancers will represent the problem area.

Predicting the effects of vaccine development

Within a 100-year timeframe, many of these ideas will seem clumsy; third and fourth generation developments will then be in use. Special attention will have to be given to noninjectable vaccines—no one wants their babies to become pincushions.

Vaccine combinations will become increasingly important. Some companies are already working on a sevenvalent vaccine against diphtheria, pertussis, tetanus, poliomyelitis, hepatitis B, Hib and meningococcus C all mixed together. A measles-mumps-rubella-chickenpox vaccine is already on the horizon. There is little doubt that a century from now, infants will be protected against most of today's most prevalent infectious diseases and even more.

How many of these diseases will we eradicate completely? The Pan American Health Organization has targeted measles as the next one for the Americas and has already made tremendous progress toward that goal. Given the problems encountered with polio eradication efforts in Africa and South Asia, global control of measles may be more realistic than total eradication. In principle, however, any microorganism against which there is a highly effective vaccine, which has no animal reservoir, and which (unlike tetanus and anthrax) does not persist long term in soil or water, is eradicable.

Vaccine combinations will become increasingly important. . . . A measles-mumps-rubella-chickenpox vaccine is already on the horizon.

The two major challenges are cost and the fact that an organism against which infants are not being immunized because it has been eradicated, such as smallpox, could be used for bioterrorism. Short of eradication, it is encouraging to note how rapidly a disease can be brought under control. For example, in Taiwan the widespread use of hepatitis B vaccine has dramatically lowered the carrier rate and has already diminished the incidence of liver cancer in relevant cohorts.

A golden century?

In a world sobered by the . . . Sept. 11, 2001, [terrorist attacks] it is no longer naïve to hope that grave social inequities around the globe will finally receive the attention they deserve. There is growing recognition that a reservoir of communicable disease in any country represents a global threat, given the extent of international travel. Prevention of infection is not only better than cure, it is much cheaper.

Yet for the splendid examples of Rotary International and Bill and Melinda Gates to be followed more extensively, one additional realization is needed. That is the nexus between health and economic development. In the words of Harvard economist Jeffrey D. Sachs and his colleagues: "The linkages of health to poverty reduction and to long-term economic growth are powerful, much stronger than is generally understood. The burden of disease in some low-income regions stands as a stark barrier to economic growth."

Sachs estimates that $30 billion per year of additional donor support could save 8 million lives each year and provide direct economic benefits of $186 billion per year. Over the next 100 years, that adds up to truly astounding progress for the human race.

15

Technological Advances Are Key to Controlling Infectious Diseases

Anthony S. Fauci

Anthony S. Fauci has been director of the National Institute of Allergy and Infectious Diseases (NIAID), within the National Institutes of Health, in Bethesda, Maryland, since 1984. He is widely recognized for his contributions to the understanding of the mechanism of HIV.

Successfully combating infectious diseases in the twenty-first century will depend on continual and rapid technological advance and scientific discovery. An array of new technologies are expected to be enormously helpful. Synthetic chemistry, robotics, and computer modeling will facilitate drug design. Also, computer models will be useful in predicting the course of microbial transmission. Information technology will facilitate the exchange of information about infectious disease among nations. Perhaps most important are two aspects of genomics: First is microbial gene sequencing, which aids in the development of diagnostics, therapeutic drugs, and vaccines by exposing vulnerabilities in a pathogen's genetic makeup; second is the human genome project, which will help researchers understand the vulnerabilities and disease mechanisms in the human host.

Critical to our ability to meet the challenges of infectious diseases in the 21st century is the continual and rapid evolution of the scientific and technological advances that serve as the foundation for the response of the public health enterprise to established, emerging, and reemerging diseases. For the discipline of infectious diseases, the application of functional genomics and proteomics will be a critical component of this science base and will draw from the sequencing not only of the human genome but also of a wide array of microbial pathogens. The areas of synthetic chemistry and robotics will greatly facilitate drug design and high-throughput screening of potential antimicrobial candidates. Computer and mathematical modeling likewise will prove useful in drug design and will also provide predictive models of microbial transmission. The field of molecular epidemiology will allow more precise delineation of microbial transmission and virulence patterns. Genetic epidemiology will lead to greater insights into host susceptibility at the individual and population levels. Finally, the rapidly advancing field of information technology will have a great impact on the field of infectious diseases in the 21st century, because rapid access and exchange of information among developed and developing nations will be critical to the overall success of any global health program.

Microbial gene sequencing

Although we have entered the 21st century armed with an ever-expanding array of technological advances to meet the current and future challenges of microbial pathogens, the microbial world is extraordinarily diverse and possesses an adaptive capacity that in many respects matches our technological capabilities. Microbes are an important part of the external and internal environment of the human species. Indeed, microbial species constitute [approximately] 60% of the Earth's biomass, but [less than] 0.5% of the estimated 2–3 billion microbial species have been identified. Microbes preceded animals and plants on Earth by [over] 3 billion years, and although only a minute fraction of all microbial species are real or potential pathogens for the human host, these pathogens continue to emerge and reemerge.

One of the most important recent technological advances in infectious diseases research has been the ability to rapidly sequence the entire genome of microbial pathogens. This capability will be a critical component of 21st century strategies for the development of diagnostics, therapeutics, and vaccines against currently recognized as well as emerging pathogens. Indeed, the microbial genome sequencing project will likely have as great an impact on the field of infectious diseases as the human genome project will on the entire field of medicine, including infectious diseases.

Critical to our ability to meet the challenges of infectious diseases in the 21st century is the continual and rapid evolution of . . . scientific and technological advances.

The first sequence of a human pathogen was obtained for *Haemophilus influenzae* in 1995. Subsequently, the pace of microbial genome sequencing has been extraordinary. As of January 2001, the sequencing of [approximately] 50 microbial genomes had been completed. It is projected that within 2–4 years, the complete sequencing of an additional 100 microbial species will be available. . . . The ability to sequence and perform sequence analysis rapidly on microbial species has resulted from the development and application of novel sequencing and computational techniques. The bold and successful application of the whole-genome "shotgun" sequencing technique used to determine the complete genome sequence of *H. in-*

fluenzae has revolutionized the field of genome sequencing.

The real and potential advantages of a microbial genomics approach to diagnostics, therapeutics, and vaccines are already being realized despite the fact that only [approximately] 50% of the genes of already sequenced microbes have tentatively assigned functions. When the functions of the remaining 50% of genes of these microbes become known, it is likely that some proportion of these will provide medically applicable insights. Determination of the function of these genes should assume a high priority in the post-sequencing, functional genomics era of the first decade of the 21st century.

The host: the human genome project and infectious diseases

The discipline of infectious diseases is centered around the study of the microbes, the host, or the interaction between the two. The completion of a working draft of the sequence of the entire human genome and the subsequent assignment of function to the 30,000–40,000 human genes, which is projected to occur over a period of several years, will have an enormous impact on the entire field of medicine. This will clearly be the case in the discipline of infectious diseases, as well as that of immunology, a large component of which represents the host response to invading microbes. The ability to examine across the entire human genome the expression of the full menu of host factors involved in the response to a microbial pathogen will provide unprecedented opportunities to understand disease pathogenesis. . . .

The availability of sequences of the entire genomes of non-human species that have a considerable degree of homology with humans will greatly facilitate the task of assigning function to the human genes as they are identified. Species such as the mouse, rat, zebrafish, [and fruitfly], among others, whose genomes have and will be sequenced will serve as invaluable tools for experimentation on the function of a wide array of genes. Among these will surely be a variety of genes whose expression is directly or indirectly involved in host defense mechanisms against pathogenic microbes. Thus, the era of genomics will affect the study of infectious diseases from a number of standpoints, including the availability of the genomic sequences of the microbes in question, the human host species, and a variety of animal species that will serve as models for experimentation and delineation of pathogenic processes associated with infection by microbial pathogens.

Vaccinology in the 21st century

The impact of vaccinology on the public health in the 20th century has been enormous. Without question, vaccines have been our most powerful tools for preventing disease, disability, and death and controlling health care costs. The evolution of the field of vaccinology has been driven by the development of enabling technologies, such as detoxification methodologies, the use of a variety of tissue culture systems to propagate microbes, and the new biotechnology of the last quarter of the 20th century, particularly that of recombinant DNA. The use of the currently available and future technologies in the 21st century promises to provide a renaissance in an already vital field. As mentioned above, the availability of the annotated sequences of the entire genomes of virtually all of the microbial pathogens will allow for the identification of a wide array of new antigens for vaccine targets. In the 21st century, vaccines derived from microbial genome–based expression of candidate antigens will be widely used. In addition to the traditional live attenuated and whole killed vaccines, concepts that are currently being actively pursued are recombinant proteins, conjugated vaccines, pseudovirions, replicons, vectored vaccines, "naked" DNA vaccines, microencapsulated vaccines, and edible vaccines. . . .

The microbial genome sequencing project will likely have as great an impact on the field of infectious diseases as the human genome project will on the entire field of medicine.

Despite the enormous successes of vaccines in decreasing the burden of morbidity and mortality caused by a variety of pathogens worldwide, continual frustration has resulted from the fact there are still millions of deaths from vaccine-preventable diseases worldwide. This is largely caused by the failure to implement vaccine delivery programs in a number of developing countries. As advanced technologies allow for the development of new vaccines against microbes for which no vaccines currently exist and improved vaccines against microbes for which a vaccine currently does exist, it is imperative that a vigorous effort is mounted to assure the delivery of such vaccines for the populations at risk.

Global health

Global health has long been a subject of intense interest and an area of commitment for a relatively small proportion of the biomedical research and public health communities in the United States. Over the past decade, this interest has become more universal and will become even more intensified in the 21st century. Although humanitarian concerns alone should have spurred such an interest, it was other factors that precipitated an acceleration of involvement in global health issues. The globalization of our economy has led to an unprecedented dependence on the economic and political stability of our trading partners. The economic and political stability of a nation is heavily influenced by the general health of that nation. The AIDS epidemic in less developed countries, particularly in sub-Saharan Africa, is a cogent example of this tenet; the same can be said for countries with a high prevalence of endemic malaria, tuberculosis, diarrheal diseases, and a wide range of parasitic diseases.

The globalization of health problems and their relevance to the United States have been brought emphatically to the attention of the American public with the HIV/AIDS epidemic. Although first recognized in the United States, HIV/AIDS is now predominantly a disease of developing countries. The scientific and public health response to HIV/AIDS in the United Sates, to which I will refer as "the AIDS model," provides important scientific and policy lessons that should be considered in our approach to other diseases of high global health impact.

The AIDS model

There have been [more than] 750,000 reported cases of AIDS in the United States and [more than] 430,000 deaths. Despite dramatic decreases in the infection rate, the number of new infections has plateaued at an unacceptably high level of 40,000 per year since the early 1990s. Nonetheless, the importance and speed of research advances that have been made since the disease was first recognized in the summer of 1981 have been breathtaking and unprecedented. Within 3 years of recognition of this new disease, the etiologic agent was identified and causality proven. A simple and accurate diagnostic test was available for screening blood donors and populations in general. Pathogenic mechanisms of HIV disease have been extensively delineated. There are currently 17 antiretroviral drugs available for the treatment of HIV disease, and these together with earlier and better treatment and prophylaxis of opportunistic diseases has led to a striking decrease in the AIDS-related death rate [since 1995]. Many of these drugs were approved by the U.S. Food and Drug Administration with unprecedented speed. Furthermore, a number of vaccine candidates are in various stages of clinical trials. Government and private organizations mobilized quickly and effectively for the care of HIV-infected persons. Education and behavioral modification efforts have contributed to considerable progress in the prevention of HIV infection, although continued and heightened vigilance is essential, because the successes with therapy have led to an unfortunate increase in risky behavior among certain groups, such as young men who have sex with men.

The evolution of the field of vaccinology has been driven by the development of enabling technologies, . . . particularly that of recombinant DNA.

These striking advances would not have occurred without the extraordinary investment in resources for biomedical research at the National Institutes of Health. In addition, major investments have been made in the public health arenas of education, behavioral modification, prevention measures, and care of HIV-infected persons. In fiscal year 2000, U.S. Department of Health and Human Services funding for AIDS research and services exceeded $8.5 billion. These investments were made possible only by the consistent bipartisan commitment of several administrations and congresses to support such endeavors. The paradigm was highly successful: a major domestic public health problem was met with a major investment of public resources, and the results in the United States and other industrialized nations were striking. However, in the last few years of the 20th century, it became apparent that the toll in suffering and death from HIV/AIDS in developing nations was enormous and dwarfed that in the United States. HIV/AIDS had evolved into a true global health catastrophe. Furthermore, the global impact of AIDS began to call greater attention to the fact that other diseases, such as malaria and tuberculosis, had been having a similar impact in developing nations for centuries. Indeed, in certain countries in sub-Saharan Africa, the "big three" of HIV/AIDS, malaria, and tuberculosis account for [over] 50% of all deaths. Compared with HIV/AIDS, relatively few research and public health resources were committed to these latter diseases by the United States and other developed nations. The question arises whether we can accomplish in malaria and tuberculosis research what has been accomplished in AIDS research. Almost certainly an infusion of dollars into malaria and tuberculosis research, analogous to the "AIDS model," would yield advances similar to those associated with HIV/AIDS research. Obviously, effective vaccines for all 3 of these diseases would be the ultimate accomplishment of a heightened research effort and would have an enormous impact on global health. However, implementation of such advances would be extremely problematic in many developing nations under the current economic conditions and with the lack of adequate health care infrastructure. In a different era, this would have been seen as an insurmountable problem, or at least someone else's problem. Today, however, global health problems, particularly those related to infectious diseases, are beginning to be perceived by political leaders in the United States and in other nations as a threat to destabilize the world. . . .

It is noteworthy that the area of science that contributed most obviously to foreign policy in the 20th century was the physical sciences related to nuclear weapons, the cold war, and the race for space exploration. It appears that the growing forces of globalization together with the fact that the health of nations is critical for economic and political stability will lead to an increasing appreciation in the 21st century of the role of biological sciences and global health, particularly with regard to infectious diseases, in the development and execution of foreign policy.

The 21st century will see an ever-increasing emphasis on infectious diseases, both because of the certainty that emerging and reemerging diseases will continue to challenge us and because globalization has led to an increased awareness of and commitment to addressing the terrible burden of infectious diseases in developing nations. Indeed, global health with an emphasis on infectious diseases is gradually assuming an important role in the foreign policy agenda of the United States and other developed nations.

Organizations to Contact

The editors have compiled the following list of organizations concerned with the issues debated in this book. The descriptions are derived from materials provided by the organizations. All have publications or information available for interested readers. The list was compiled on the date of publication of the present volume; names, addresses, phone and fax numbers, and e-mail addresses may change. Be aware that many organizations take several weeks or longer to respond to inquiries, so allow as much time as possible.

Center for Infectious Disease Research and Policy (CIDRAP)
University of Minnesota Academic Health Center
420 Delaware St. SE, MMC 263, Minneapolis, MN 55455
(612) 626-6770 • fax: (612) 626-6783
e-mail: cidrap@umn.edu • Web site: www.cidrap.umn.edu

A program based at the University of Minnesota Academic Health Center, CIDRAP is a research and international advisory group focusing on issues of public health and bioterrorism preparedness, infectious disease information systems, and vaccine and antimicrobial safeguards. Publicly and privately funded, the center conducts original, interdisciplinary research into the epidemiology, control, and prevention of infectious diseases and disseminates authoritative information on current disease threats on its Web site, which is updated daily.

Centers for the Study of Bioterrorism and Emerging Infections (CSB&EI)
3545 Lafayette Ave., Suite 300, St. Louis, MO 63104
(314) 977-8257 • fax: (314) 977-1674
Web site: www.slu.edu/colleges/sph/csbei

The St. Louis University School of Public Health hosts these research centers, whose useful Web sites provide descriptions of infectious agents and their transmission; links to medical and regulatory references, articles, and bibliographies; a list of case studies pertaining to infectious disease outbreaks; and information on treating exposure to biological weapons.

Global Alliance for Vaccines and Immunization (GAVI)
601 Thirteenth St. NW, Washington, DC 20005
(201) 628-4910 • fax: (201) 628-4909
Web site: www.vaccinealliance.org

An alliance of private-sector philanthropic organizations and governmental donors, GAVI's mission is to improve children's health worldwide via increased access to vaccines. It finances vaccination and public health programs in poor countries and advocates accelerated research and development programs for new vaccines. The GAVI Web site offers status reports on research into and availability of vaccines against influenza, yellow fever, rotovirus, measles, HIV, encephalitis, malaria, and tuberculosis, as well as frequent press releases and progress reports on its public health initiatives.

National Center for Infectious Diseases (NCID)
Office of Health Communication, Centers for Disease Control and Prevention
Mailstop C-14, 1600 Clifton Rd., Atlanta, GA 30333
e-mail: ncid@cdc.gov • Web site: www.cdc.gov

The NCID is one of the twelve divisions of the Centers for Disease Control
and Prevention, the federal agency charged with preventing and controlling
diseases and responding to public health emergencies. The center publishes
Emerging Infectious Diseases: A Strategy for the 21st Century; the 2003 Institute
of Medicine study *Microbial Threats to Health: Emergence, Detection, and Response;* and the monthly online journal *Emerging Infectious Diseases,* which
tracks and analyzes disease trends. Its Web site features the link "Need Help
on a School Project?" connecting students to a comprehensive list of useful
resources and publications.

National Foundation for Infectious Diseases (NFID)
4733 Bethesda Ave., Suite 750, Bethesda, MD 20814
(301) 656-0003 • fax: (301) 907-0878
e-mail: info@nfid.org • Web site: www.nfid.org

The foundation is a nonprofit philanthropic organization that supports disease research through grants and fellowships and educates the public about
infectious disease and the importance of immunization. It publishes a newsletter, *Double Helix,* and its Web site contains the "Virtual Library of Diseases."

National Institute of Allergy and Infectious Diseases (NIAID)
National Institutes of Health (NIH)
Office of Communications and Public Liaison
31 Center Drive, MSC 2520, Building 31, Bethesda, MD 20892-2520
(301) 496-5717
e-mail: ldoepel@nih.gov • Web site: www.niaid.nih.gov

NIAID, a component of the federal National Institutes of Health, conducts
and supports basic research into immune-mediated and allergic diseases,
AIDS, emerging diseases, and vaccines under its director, Anthony S. Fauci.
The institute supports a network of investigators in academic and industry
laboratories around the world and offers both scientific and nonscientific
summer internships to students at its home facility in Maryland. Its many free
publications include newsletters, reports on clinical drug trials, and summaries such as the *NIAID Global Health Research Plan for HIV/AIDS, Malaria,
and Tuberculosis.*

U.S. Army Medical Research Institute of Infectious Diseases (USAMRIID)
Attn: MCMR-UIZ-R
1425 Porter St., Fort Detrick, Frederick, MD 21702-5011
e-mail: USAMRIIDweb@amedd.army.mil • Web site: www.usamriid.army.mil

USAMRIID is the leading medical research laboratory and largest biocontainment laboratory in the Department of Defense for the study of hazardous diseases. Its research focuses on both biological warfare threats and naturally occurring infectious diseases that require special containment. The institute
maintains a library of scientific and educational publications available to the
general public on its Web site, focusing on bacteriology, immunology, and
pathogen/toxin identification. The institute's Web site also provides interesting descriptions of the laboratory design and equipment that enables researchers to safely investigate Biosafety Level 3 and 4 pathogens.

World Health Organization (WHO)
525 Twenty-Third St. NW, Washington, DC 20037
(202) 974-3000 • fax: (202) 974-3663
e-mail: postmaster@paho.org • Web site: www.who.int

WHO is the United Nations specialized agency for health, based in Geneva, Switzerland. It monitors and responds to disease outbreaks around the world, sponsors international conferences on public health threats, issues traveler's advisories and vaccination requirements, and develops strategies for improving human health such as the "3 × 5 Initiative," which aims to provide medical treatment for 3 million people infected with HIV in the developing world by 2005. It publishes the annual *World Health Report*, the monthly *Bulletin of the World Health Organization*, and the *WHO Weekly Epidemiological Record*, which compiles data and statistics on current disease trends.

Bibliography

Books

Tony Barnett and Alan Whiteside — *AIDS in the Twenty-first Century: Disease and Globalization.* New York: Palgrave Macmillan, 2002.

Wayne Biddle — *A Field Guide to Germs.* Rev. ed. New York: Knopf, 2002.

Barry R. Bloom and Paul-Henri Lambert, eds. — *The Vaccine Book.* London: Academic, 2002.

Board on Global Health — *Microbial Threats to Health: Emergence, Detection, and Response,* a report of the Institute of Medicine of the National Academies. Ed. Mark S. Smolinski, Margaret A. Hamburg, and Joshua Lederberg. Washington, DC: National Academies Press, 2003.

Rob DeSalle, ed. — *Epidemic! The World of Infectious Disease.* New York: New Press, 1999.

Madeline Drexler — *Secret Agents: The Menace of Emerging Infections.* Washington, DC: Joseph Henry, an imprint of National Academies Press, 2002.

Laurie Garrett — *Betrayal of Trust: The Collapse of Global Public Health.* New York: Hyperion, 2000.

Susan Hunter — *Black Death: AIDS in Africa.* New York: Palgrave Macmillan, 2003.

Scott P. Layne et al., eds. — *Firepower in the Lab: Automation in the Fight Against Infectious Diseases and Bioterrorism.* Washington, DC: Joseph Henry, 2001.

Elinor Levy and Mark Fischetti — *The New Killer Diseases: How the Alarming Evolution of Mutant Germs Threatens Us All.* New York: Crown, 2003.

Stuart B. Levy — *The Antibiotic Paradox: How the Misuse of Antibiotics Destroys Their Curative Powers.* Rev. ed. New York: Perseus, 2002.

Judith Miller, Stephen Engelberg, and William J. Broad — *Germs: Biological Weapons and America's Secret War.* New York: Simon and Schuster, 2001.

Michael B.A. Oldstone — *Viruses, Plagues, and History.* New York: Oxford University Press, 1998.

Jonathan B. Tucker — *Scourge: The Once and Future Threat of Smallpox.* New York: Grove, 2002.

Periodicals

Lawrence K. Altman — "What Is the Next Plague?" *New York Times*, November 11, 2003.

Seth Borenstein — "World Sees an Explosion in New Infectious Diseases," *San Jose Mercury News*, May 4, 2003.

John Carey — "One Scary Bug: A New Virus from Asia [SARS] Raises a Host of Unnerving Questions," *Business Week*, April 14, 2003.

Geoffrey Cowley — "How Progress Makes Us Sick: Advances That Make Life More Comfortable Can Also Make It More Dangerous," *Newsweek*, May 5, 2003.

Madeline Drexler — "The Germ Front: Experts Differ over Whether Chemical and Biological Warfare Pose a Mass Threat—but They Agree That We Need a Stronger Public Health Response," *American Prospect*, November 5, 2001.

Peter Duesberg — "The African AIDS Epidemic: New and Contagious—or—Old Under a New Name?" Duesberg on AIDS, June 22, 2000. http://207.201.169.183/subject/africa2.html.

Emerging Infectious Diseases — Special issue on bioterrorism-related anthrax, October 2002. www.cdc.gov.

Hilary French — "Travel and Trade: Hidden Threats," *USA Today Magazine*, March 2001.

Anne Hardy — "Animals, Disease, and Man: Making Connections," *Perspectives in Biology and Medicine*, vol. 46, no. 2, Spring 2003.

Intergovernmental Panel on Climate Change, United Nations Environment Programme and World Meteorological Organization — "Human Health," *Climate Change 2001: Impacts, Adaptation, and Vulnerability*, 2001. www.grida.no/climate/ipcc_tar/wg2/347.htm.

Claudia Kalb — "Tracking SARS," *Newsweek*, April 28, 2003.

John Lee — "Tuberculosis, the White Plague: For Centuries It Had Been the Scourge of Humanity, but Antibiotics Seemed to Have It Licked. Then Along Came HIV," *New Scientist*, November 9, 2002.

John MacGregor — "Set a Bug to Catch a Bug: As the Power of Antibiotics Wanes, Viruses That Hijack Bacteria and Smash Them to Pieces Could Be the Answer to Our Prayers," *New Scientist*, April 5, 2003.

Laura MacLehose, Martin McKee, and Julius Weinberg — "Responding to the Challenge of Communicable Disease in Europe," *Science*, March 15, 2002.

Kenan Malik — "Don't Panic: It's Safer than You Think," *New Statesman*, October 8, 2001.

Declan McCullagh   "Something's in the Air: Liberties in the Face of SARS and Other Infectious Diseases," *Reason*, August 2003.

Tim McGirk and   "Stalking a Killer: In the Time It Takes the Average
Susan Jakes   Person to Read This Story, 40 Asians Will Die of AIDS,"
    Time, September 30, 2002.

New England Journal   Special issue on smallpox and smallpox vaccination,
of Medicine   January 30, 2003.

Fred Pearce   "Pests and Pestilence: Why Humans Are More Vulnerable than Ever to Animal-Borne Diseases," *Foreign Policy*, July/August 2003.

John Pickrell   "Aerial War Against Disease: Satellite Tracking of Epidemics Is Soaring," *Science News*, April 6, 2002.

Douglas Steinberg   "Antiterror Agenda Promotes Ebola Vaccine and Immunotherapy: Animals Survive with Treatment, but Will Humans?" *Scientist*, July 8, 2002.

Joel L. Swerdlow   "Living with Microbes," *Wilson Quarterly*, vol. 26, no. 2,
and Ari D. Johnson   Spring 2002.

UNAIDS   "AIDS Epidemic Update: Sub-Saharan Africa," Joint United Nations Programme on HIV/AIDS, December 2003. www.unaids.org/wad/2003/Epiupdate2003_en/Epi03_04_en.htm.

Carl Zimmer   "Do Chronic Diseases Have an Infectious Root?" *Science*, vol. 293, no. 5537, September 14, 2001.

Web site

Epidemic! The World   www.amnh.org/exhibitions/epidemic/index.html.
of Infectious Disease   Originally a highly praised traveling exhibition mounted in 1999 by the American Museum of Natural History, this site traces the emergence, control, and prevention of infectious disease using examples such as the hantavirus outbreak in the U.S. Southwest. It contains a glossary and a comprehensive list of online resources for further research.

Index

DATE DUE

	2005		

#47-0108 Peel Off Pressure Sensitive